What readers are saying about this book

The death of a child In this real-life story, for her family to rem methods for helping ot marital discord and pro......... ... ., ..., ... dedication and love for one another, and reaching out to others, has sustained the Mayhalls through this crisis. They have become mentors, healers and models for accepting tragedy without bitterness or losing faith.

> *Evelyn Freeman, former Coordinator of Child*
> *Development Programs, Seattle Public Schools*

A grief management guide, a humane reminder and a family memoir all rolled into one sweet and moving story told with great compassion and honesty.
> *Elizabeth Tobiasson, New Hampshire Artisan*

A personal story of loss and recovery that depicts the human condition in which all life is held captive to circumstances beyond human control. The author attempts to "Bridge" a concrete experience of death and its aftermath by creating a plausible abstract phenomenon – that Heaven is a real place where past and present join together; where the five people you meet in Heaven become a reality. Bridging the gulf between the concrete and the abstract is the power of love.
> *Dave Eekhoff, Presbyterian Minister, Pastoral*
> *Counselor, Marriage and Family Therapist*

This book demonstrates the importance of a strong network of family and friends to enhance the grieving family's resilience and their ability to grow stronger through tragedy while moving forward on life's journey. This is a resource that can help a child or parent deal with loss.
> *Nancy Henderlite, Elementary School Counselor*

A mother's eulogy and a treatise on coping with which any family that has lost a child could identify.
> *Richard Holt, M.D. Pediatric Hospitalist*

The author invites you to share a mother's personal search for "normal" after tragedy suddenly turns her life upside-down. She allows the reader to travel her journey through grief after the death of her child, discovering how hope and faith make living bearable. Lesson: Take advantage of joy! Glean it from wherever you can! Let the unchangeable past be what it is.
> *Dusty Westall, Early Childhood Educator*

A revealing story of how a family in crisis changed and emerged stronger and more loving after the death of a child.
Mike Garcia, Funeral Director

Many families fall apart after the loss of a child. The Mayhall family grew stronger together through their struggles with grief and stress. The author adds an important dimension of spirituality and hope by interweaving an account of the child's new life in Heaven.
Noel Phillips, D.Min., BCC Hospital Chaplain

This book can be a catalyst for bereaved ones to focus on life rather than death. It has generational appeal – children and grandchildren would enjoy it, too.
Jess Grable, Leader, The Compassionate Friends

So often we talk about the birth of a child giving all the "vital statistics," but how difficult to put a voice to the death of a child with all the "vital statistics." Mayhall's frankness in letting us view the despair, and later life renewal, feels "like family."
Geri Eekhoff, Hospice Nurse and Counselor

A heartwarming portrayal of Heaven as a safe, homey place for children who died at a young age. It provides a sense of relief and acceptance for parents of all children.
Pat Conrad, Teacher

Combine grief, faith and fluency and you have a story that speaks to all parents who have known what it is to lose a child. It is also a story about Heaven that will appeal to any child's imagination as well as to any adult who has a childlike faith.
Bob Postma, B.A., B.D., Pastoral Counselor, retired

A mother's memorial that provides words of comfort and healing for middle school to adult readers who are exploring grief, have lost a loved one, or fear death.
Julie Farnam, Licensed Clinical Social Worker

The Bridge Is Love

A Journey Through Grief to Joy After the Death of a Child

A Memoir / Novel

by

Cheron J. Mayhall, Ph.D.

Cover Illustration
Katrina Mayhall Wyman

© Copyright 2005 Cheron J. Mayhall, PhD.
Cover Illustration by Katrina Mayhall Wyman.
All rights reserved. No part of this publication may be reproduced, stored in a retrieval system, or transmitted, in any form or by any means, electronic, mechanical, photocopying, recording, or otherwise, without the written prior permission of the author.

Note for Librarians: A cataloguing record for this book is available from Library and Archives Canada at www.collectionscanada.ca/amicus/index-e.html
ISBN 1-4120-6328-0

Printed in Victoria, BC, Canada. Printed on paper with minimum 30% recycled fibre. Trafford's print shop runs on "green energy" from solar, wind and other environmentally-friendly power sources.

Offices in Canada, USA, Ireland and UK
This book was published *on-demand* in cooperation with Trafford Publishing. On-demand publishing is a unique process and service of making a book available for retail sale to the public taking advantage of on-demand manufacturing and Internet marketing. On-demand publishing includes promotions, retail sales, manufacturing, order fulfilment, accounting and collecting royalties on behalf of the author.

Book sales for North America and international:
Trafford Publishing, 6E–2333 Government St.,
Victoria, BC V8T 4P4 CANADA
phone 250 383 6864 (toll-free 1 888 232 4444)
fax 250 383 6804; email to orders@trafford.com
Book sales in Europe:
Trafford Publishing (UK) Limited, 9 Park End Street, 2nd Floor
Oxford, UK OX1 1HH UNITED KINGDOM
phone 44 (0)1865 722 113 (local rate 0845 230 9601)
facsimile 44 (0)1865 722 868; info.uk@trafford.com
Order online at:
trafford.com/05-1239

10 9 8 7 6 5 4 3 2

Permission to Reprint

The Bridge of San Luis Rey by Thornton Wilder, Copyright 1927 by Albert and Charles Boni, Inc.; renewed 1955 by Thornton Wilder. Current rights controlled by HarperCollins Publishers.

Loneliness and Love by Clark Moustakas, Copyright 1972 by Clark Moustakas. Simon & Schuster, Inc.

Death be Not Proud by John Gunther, Copyright 1949 by John Gunther. Copyright Renewed 1976 by Jane Perry Gunther. HarperCollins Publishers.

The Bridge Is Love

Dedication

In loving memory of Scotty,
Alex, Grandma Gratia,
R.W. Wettleson and Albert Schweitzer
(The first five people I hope to meet in Heaven)

Acknowledgments

In 1967, my professor in Ohio, Don Carew, wrote: "Cheron… You have a way of saying things…of sharing your self that adds meaning to the lives of others…You must continue to write…not in the stilted jargon of professional journals but in your spontaneous, thoughtful, beautiful, open way that will enrich the lives of readers." I thank Don for his mandate which has inspired me through the years. Likewise I am indebted to my high school journalism teacher, who changed my life by insisting that I read a wide variety of books, contemplate their meaning, and write, write, write with conscience and creativity. You will meet him in the pages of this book.

The women in my Port Townsend writers group deserve my enormous gratitude, especially Mary Brunner, Dusty Westall and Evelyn Freeman who were my most persistent critics and supporters from the story's inception through its publication. Willean Hornbeck applied her careful eye to final proofreading. Many qualified peer reviewers in the helping professions provided valuable and constructive input to improve the final draft. A number of bereaved parents, some leaders of Compassionate Friends chapters, cried and rejoiced knowingly as they read these pages and validated my thoughts, feelings and hopes. I am indebted to them all.

My thanks to Simon & Schuster, Inc. and HarperCollins Publishers for granting permission to reprint copyrighted materials.

I've written this book because I felt compelled or "called" to do so. It has been a spiritual journey guided and goaded along by God. It is a token of my gratitude for His constant presence in my life. It is my fervent hope that the account of my family's journey through grief will provide assurances and comfort to all who grieve the loss of a beloved. This my vision that the eternal connectedness conquers death and overcomes despair.

I thank my husband, Bill, for his support and constancy throughout nearly forty years of marriage and childrearing. We have endured many challenges together and grown stronger and more in love through it all. Finally, special thanks to my artistic, younger daughter, Katie, who has captured the beauty and essence of this story in her cover illustration.

Contents

Primary Characters		13
Preface		15
Chapter 1	The Accident	17
Chapter 2	Day One, Saturday	25
Chapter 3	Day Two, Sunday a.m.	31
Chapter 4	Heavenly Home	33
Chapter 5	Day Two, Sunday p.m.	40
Chapter 6	The Funeral	47
Chapter 7	The Memorial Service	51
Chapter 8	A Heavenly Roommate	55
Chapter 9	The Solace Stone	59
Chapter 10	Scotty's Life in Oregon	63
Chapter 11	Uncle Bob and the Treehouse	66
Chapter 12	Returning to Corvallis; Confronting Death's Realities	74
Chapter 13	Yellow Mercedes	80
Chapter 14	Memories and Keepsakes	83
Chapter 15	The First Day of School	87
Chapter 16	Life Goes On	92
Chapter 17	An Afternoon with Jesus	96
Chapter 18	Dreams, Images, Searching for Answers	106
Chapter 19	Praying for Babies	112
Chapter 20	Autumn and Halloween	113
Chapter 21	Uncle Bob and Mom	118
Chapter 22	The Compassionate Friends	122
Chapter 23	Thanksgiving, Green Peas and Football	128

Chapter 24	Little Beavers Christmas	133
Chapter 25	A Blessed Event	136
Chapter 26	The Joy of Christmas	142
Chapter 27	Bundle of Joy	146
Chapter 28	Scotty's Life in New Mexico	149
Chapter 29	Laura Makes the Rounds	154
Chapter 30	Valentine's Day	157
Chapter 31	Lunch with Albert	158
Chapter 32	Rhonda and Remembrance	164
Chapter 33	More Tragedy on 99W	168
Chapter 34	Baptism and Birthday	170
Chapter 35	Springtime	174
Chapter 36	Deaf, not Dead!	177
Chapter 37	Playground Dedication Day	180
Chapter 38	September Surprise	183

Postscript	185
Bibliography	191
A Path through Grief Work to Healing	192
Quick Order Form	193
About the Author	194

Primary Characters

In Heaven

Scotty... Bill and Cheron's second son
Uncle Alex/Unk... Scotty's uncle; Cheron's brother
GG... Scotty's great-grandmother; Cheron's maternal grandmother
Uncle Bob... Scotty's heavenly neighbor; Cheron's high school teacher/mentor
Steve... Scotty's heavenly roommate
Jesus... God's "only begotten son"
Albert Schweitzer... Jungle doctor & Nobel Peace Prize winner; Cheron's hero

On Earth

Bill and Cheron... Scotty's parents
Phillip... Scotty's big brother
Auntie Alice, Auntie Mary, Auntie Connie... Cheron's sisters; Scotty's aunts
David, Daniel and Darren Kelly... Auntie Alice's sons; Scotty's cousins
Grandmother and Granddaddy... Bill's parents; Scotty's Texas grandparents
Granny... Cheron's mother; Scotty's Seattle grandma
Art and Sue... Scotty's godparents
Satsuki Tomine... Cheron's college friend
"Gramma Edna" and "Grampa Larry"... Mayhalls' next-door neighbors
Hal and Judy Boyd... Mayhall family friends
John Chester... Mayhall family friend
Al and Jan East... Little Beavers Preschool owners
Rhonda... Scotty's preschool teacher
Heidi and Sonya... Mayhall family dogs

Preface

This book is a true story with a novel twist to enhance the reader's appreciation for and endurance of the subject matter. It chronicles the pathos of a family striving to recover from the sudden death of a young child…my child. Growing and changing through the pain of loneliness and loss, the characters discover the emergence of new joys and strengths. Hope and faith make the tragedy bearable, even if incomprehensible and unacceptable in our earthly ways of perceiving. While we can grasp the idea of "everything in its season," our spirits must embrace a sense of mystery if we are to thrive in the aftermath of a loved one's death. We are challenged to be content with knowing that there is a circle of life, and each person who is born on this Earth occupies a unique and important place in that circle.

> …But soon we shall die and all memory of those five will have left the earth, and we ourselves shall be loved for a while and forgotten. But the love will have been enough; all those impulses of love return to the love that made them. Even memory is not necessary for love. There is a land of the living and a land of the dead and the bridge is love, the only survival, the only meaning.
>
> Thornton Wilder, *The Bridge of San Luis Rey*

My memoir provides glimpses into the "land of the dead" as well as a poignant, true narrative of people in passage through both the sacred and mundane experiences of life after unspeakable tragedy. The bridge of love between Earth and Heaven can sustain us in our sorrow and heal our wounded spirits. It is a pathway that can lead the heart to new destinations where joy and peace can be reclaimed.

Cheron Joy Mayhall
2005

1   The Accident

Everyone called me Scotty, but my full name was Thomas Joseph Scott Mayhall. It was my father's family tradition to hang at least three original names on each newborn baby. I lived on Earth exactly four years, four months and nine days before being killed in a big car crash one summer evening. That was a long time ago – July 22, 1977 – and that's where my story begins. My memories have become more vivid and my ability to tell the story gets better with each passing year.

I loved being a four-year-old in Oregon, but everything changed that July night. Back then there was less awareness about seatbelts and no laws about "buckling up" for children or adults. Being little, I needed reminding, and the seatbelt in the back was tucked away out of sight. My brother Phillip and I had never been inside the babysitter's car and, besides, we were too busy playing silly word games with her two children standing up in the front seat. None of us knew she was driving too fast on a country road to see and observe the stop sign at the highway intersection. I don't remember the crash or the car spinning and bouncing out of control.

I felt myself cradled in the arms of someone soft, though I knew it wasn't my mother. And it wasn't Eunice, the dark-skinned Sunday school teacher who loved to rock me in the big chair in our church's toddler room. She was kind of like a grandma and she made me feel warm and safe. On that July evening I was being rocked and I could hear a soft sobbing as my hair was tenderly brushed back from my forehead. The woman embracing me was shivering, or shaking, even though the air around us was hot and dry.

I thought I smelled hot metal and gasoline, like when Dad filled the tank at Ernie's station near our house. I sensed commotion around me and then heard from a distance the siren sounds of "Emergency." That was the favorite television show I watched with Phillip every week. We loved imitating our paramedic heroes, John and Roy, with our plastic fireman hats and make-believe hoses and first-aid kits.

At the accident scene, I had a strange, mixed sensation of both peace and excitement. I couldn't open my eyes or move my arms and legs but I was only half-sure that I wanted to. The comfort I was feeling made me less curious about what was happening all around me. I wanted to relax and enjoy the warmth of those gentle arms, my head nestled into that soft bosom. I felt myself sinking deeper and deeper; I wanted to sleep.

Suddenly the activity around me began increasing, with close-in sirens and many voices slightly penetrating my consciousness. Then, the back-and-forth, rocking motion changed. I realized I was in an ambulance as John and Roy from "Emergency" cared for me with all the excitement portrayed each week on our TV show. I couldn't understand what they were saying or doing, but I sensed I was safe and loved. I could feel my spirit being gently carried away from those familiar places in Oregon where I'd spent so many happy days.

I think I slept for quite awhile because I felt rested and ready for action when I woke up. After checking to see that I had all my rescue gear attached to my belts, I looked around and saw my Schwinn bicycle nearby. At first I wasn't sure it was mine because there was a kickstand, but no training wheels. Then I noticed the trademark "S" on the seat, to which I had added the letters "c-o-t-t-y" with a red Magic Marker. I thought I could see a treehouse in the distance, too, but my biggest and happiest surprise was seeing my Uncle Alex walking toward me with outstretched arms and his great, big smile. He wore a sweatshirt with "Seattle Supersonics" scrolled across it in yellow and green letters.

"Hey, Unk," I hollered, "where's your bike? Did you come to ride with me and Phillip?" His answer was to gather me up in a giant bear hug. He tousled my hair with his huge hand and said he'd been waiting for me. Then he knelt his 6'5" frame, sat me on the ground, and looked lovingly into my eyes.

"I've missed you, Scotty, all these months since I died the day before Halloween. By the way, I saw you trick-or-treating in your Frankenstein costume. You looked very scary!" Alex paused and looked me over from head to toe. " I've been missing all my kids and my nieces and nephews back on Earth. You are the youngest of the fifteen cousins...our 'little guy.' And now, for sure, you are our 'Littlest Angel'."

"Well," I said, "if I'm the littlest angel you are the biggest, giantest one I ever saw!"

I looked around behind both of us but I didn't see any wings or halos. *The Littlest Angel* by Charles Tazewell was Mom's favorite Christmas story. We had heard her read it many times during the holidays, year after year. The angels pictured in her book had great wings and were able to fly. Flying was one of the things I always wanted to do. It made me wonder if there were space ships somewhere in this place, and maybe astronauts like Neil Armstrong. I felt a little confused, but I knew that having Uncle Alex all to myself for awhile was going to be lots of fun, whether we could fly or not. He tickled and teased better than anyone in the whole world and he always seemed to love the littlest person the most. I was in heaven!

After we were worn out from laughing so hard as we played tag and hide-and-seek and airplane, we collapsed side by side on the grass. I was growing more curious about our surroundings and how we came to be together in this place. Uncle Alex snuggled me close beside him and began filling me in on what had happened while I moved between Earth and Heaven.

I told him I remembered saying goodbye to Mom and Dad in our driveway. I knew that finding a babysitter and traveling into the city for dinner with friends was a special treat for them. When the sitter arrived at our house with her six-year-old twins and teenage niece, I was thinking that the four of us little kids and our dog would head off on a great adventure in the two wooded acres we called our yard. The sitter told my folks that she first needed to drive her niece to a family farm about 20 miles away, so our trek into the forest would have to wait an hour or two. With dinner reservations and friends waiting to carpool, there was no time to switch gears or make other childcare arrangements. So my parents, Bill and Cheron, headed off in one direction, and the remaining six of us piled into the sitter's car and started south.

Uncle Alex told me how the four grown-ups had enjoyed a leisurely seafood dinner at a fancy restaurant on the riverfront. Dad had met John while they were serving weekend duty together in the National Guard. John and his wife had a couple of kids about the same ages as Phillip and me. The dads found our families had a lot in common. Having become good friends, they decided to take the moms out so they could all get better acquainted. Their friendship grew as they enjoyed crab claws, Chardonnay and conversation comparing stories, mostly about their kids.

At 10:30 they were back in John's car headed home to relieve the babysitters before midnight. John pulled into his driveway and they said their good-byes. But, before Mom and Dad could get into their car for the drive home, John's teenage sitter came out on the porch with a message. She looked very tense. Her eyes appeared enlarged. There had been an urgent phone call for Bill, my dad, from a friend at a hospital in the valley. My dad's a doctor, and he was used to being called about emergencies. "I guess the operator didn't read the call schedule," he remarked. "She should have contacted the doctor on call."

Standing around the counter in John's kitchen, the shock and horror of the phone message quickly penetrated the air like the odor of a gas leak foretelling an explosion. Dad looked across the counter at Mom and said, "Scotty's dead." Just like that. No one knew for sure what else was covered in the phone conversation, but that was the bottom line. I was dead, but Phillip was alive and he'd be okay. John offered to drive the fifty miles to the hospital. Dad wrapped his arms around Mom and escorted her to the car.

Mom burrowed her head into Dad's shoulder as he recounted what he'd learned on the phone. The accident occurred at the

Suver intersection just after 6:30 p.m., in broad daylight. Local volunteers from the rural fire station were on the scene within minutes, but it took half an hour for the ambulance to arrive. All the car's occupants were transported to the hospital. I was the only one who died. The babysitter who was driving and one of her twins had broken bones. Phillip suffered a concussion and bruises, especially where the seatbelt restraint had crossed his chest. He had remembered to buckle up.

Though desperate to get to Phillip's bedside, Mom realized she needed a "pit stop" so John drove a short distance off the highway to our house. Hearing the midnight commotion, "Gramma" Edna and "Grampa" Larry came down the road from their house next door to ours. They loved all us Mayhalls as if we were their own children and grandchildren. All our neighbors had learned hours earlier that there had been a serious accident involving two families on our hill. The police had been there but they didn't report all the details of what had happened. Edna and Larry had been praying. Now they encircled my folks to comfort and assure them that everything would be all right. "Scotty's dead," my dad blurted out. There was stunned silence followed by tears flowing down every face.

Aside from the crying sounds, everyone could hear the barking of our St. Bernard puppy, Heidi, coming from inside the house. Mom excused herself and went in through the kitchen and toward the bathroom. Heidi begged Mom to stop and pet her, seemingly confused at having been left alone into the night hours when ordinarily the family was all tucked into bed and fast asleep. Mom gathered the pup into her arms and buried her face in the soft fur, sobbing. Heidi pulled back and licked away the salty tears running down her cheeks. Heidi had been the runt in a litter of eight puppies, small enough to hold in one of Dad's hands when she came to live with us four months earlier. Now she was the same size as me, almost forty pounds, covered with lots of brown and white curls, black freckles dotting her white muzzle.

"Cheron, we need to get going, honey," Dad called from the yard. Mom regained her composure and splashed cool water from the kitchen faucet on her splotchy face. Soon they were in John's car headed south the additional 30 highway miles to the hospital.

I closed my eyes as Uncle Alex described the scenes in the hospital. It was as if he were right there inside my mom's skin and brain. I guess that's not so strange since they were brother and sister and both of them loved Phillip and me so much. Unk told me, "Your mom could hear voices speaking in hushed, secretive tones in the Emergency Room. She realized that only your dad was being directed to the place in the hospital where your body had been taken. She seemed to know instinctively the importance of seeing your body, to connect as fully and as quickly as possible with the reality of the tragedy. Your dad knew the measure of her strength and stamina and agreed that she should follow her intuition. They slipped away to the staircase and descended.

"Your small, slim body was laid out on a table in the cool basement room, showing no signs of the trauma that had stopped the last breath and the rhythmic beating of your heart. Except for a little swelling around your neck and cheeks, it just looked like you were sleeping naked and with no blanket on." I giggled at the thought of that! I'm shy, and I always slept in my pj's and loved to cover up with my favorite blanket that had space ships and astronauts on it. "She reached out and found your body cold to the touch, yet clean and soft. She caressed your slender arms and legs and laid her head on your chest. Then she kissed your eyelids, knowing now that she would never again see them open to reveal your sparkling blue eyes."

Several of my parents' friends who had been easily contacted by the on-call operator had rushed to the hospital to be with Phillip and me. They waited anxiously for my parents' arrival, but anxiety now turned to agony as they watched their friends grieve over their precious son's still body. They would have liked to intervene and take away the pain. Not possible. Uncle Alex explained, "You remember, Scotty, when your cat, Jenny, died, and when I died? All the people who love you are going to feel lost and terribly sad for awhile. They need time to get used to your not being around on Earth anymore. I'll help you understand what's going on down there and I'll teach you what I've learned about helping them find happiness again. It won't be too hard. Around here little child-angels tend to grow in wisdom and get smarter very quickly."

That reminded me of how Phillip had talked about Uncle Alex the year before when he died of cancer. Phillip told me that Unk had changed into an angel up above. Because he was a "sports nut" and loved going to basketball, football and baseball games, Phillip envisioned our uncle as having a better view of the action than even the best seat in any stadium. So I figured that maybe that had happened to me, too. Somehow I had flown up into the sky, even without wings or a rocket ship, and now I had the powers to look down to Earth and see anything I wanted to see. Just like Superman with x-ray vision.

I told my uncle as we lay there on the grass in Heaven, "I feel as close to my family as ever, only I can't touch them from here." I think I had some kind of a dream while I was getting from Oregon to Heaven. I remembered my mother's touch and her tears at the hospital. I really wanted to let her know I was okay, but she seemed to sense it anyhow. I guess that's what Mom had tried to teach Phillip and me about how all our spirits stay connected forever. Then, while our friends at the hospital looked on, feeling sad and helpless, my mom suddenly ran out of tears, stopped crying and became calm and serene. She was able to smile a tender good-bye and grab my dad's hand as they headed upstairs to check on Phillip.

"Oh, yeah," I told Uncle Alex, "I remember when Dad and Mom got to Phillip's hospital room." He didn't look so bad to me, but he was real woozy and couldn't talk straight. Mom hugged him; he moaned and opened his eyes for just a minute. He didn't have a bunch of tubes coming out of him like the kid in the next bed. Dad told Phillip he was going to be just fine and they'd all go home in a few minutes so he could get tucked into his own bed. Mom tried really hard not to cry or fuss too much, so Phillip wouldn't worry. The doctors had decided it was worth the risk to discharge Phillip so that Mom and Dad could take at least one of their sons home. Dr. Chester, the senior doctor in my dad's group, said he'd drive since John, Dad's National Guard buddy, had gone back home to be with his worried wife and to tuck his own small children safely into their beds.

    Phillip was wrapped tight in a blanket, like a mummy. Dad laid him across their laps in the back seat. Mom cradled his head and hummed a lullaby, though it was breathy because she had a knot in her throat. Dr. Chester drove like a chauffeur up in the front seat. The 30-minute trip was made in silence. Everyone was so tired and so sad, and there weren't words to change those feelings. In the car behind, Dr. Boyd and his wife, Judy, headed for our house, too. Phillip didn't even wake up when the two cars arrived in our driveway, so Dad carried him to his bed and returned to the group in the family room. Judy asked Mom if she could make some tea, but Mom couldn't seem to remember where she kept the teakettle or tea bags. They sat for a few minutes, but nobody knew what to say, except that Dr. Chester mentioned he had a good friend in the funeral business and would have him arrange to bring my body back to our hometown, Salem. It was after 4 a.m. when everyone left our house.

    That's how I recall what took place the night of the wreck. I felt sad that my family was back home without me. But suddenly I remembered that I was in this new place Uncle Alex called Heaven, and I hadn't had a chance yet to explore. "Hey, Unk, I'm going to go on a little bike ride to check this place out, okay? Can you keep an eye on what's happening back home and fill me in later?" Unk smiled and nodded so I hopped on my red and white Schwinn, amazed that I could now get my balance and ride it easily without the training wheels. I wanted to see that treehouse I'd spotted earlier, and there were some other angel-people moving about now. I hoped I'd find some kids my age to play with.

2 Day One, Saturday

Looking through his sister's eyes, Alex could feel her enormous pain as she quietly, but deliberately, closed the door to Scotty's bedroom, choking back the tears that had started flowing again. She avoided gazing in at the many little-boy belongings so full of Scotty's spirit. The well-worn, hand-me-down cowboy boots they'd brought home from the hospital, parachute man, Honey Bear, the Emergency fire hat and one of the ropes Scotty used for his "rescue missions." There would be time to sort through the mementos later, but now she needed to rest and be there beside Bill in his quiet sorrow. As they embraced each other under the sheets, it seemed they couldn't get close enough. Their physical and emotional union finally gave some solace and Bill drifted off to sleep. She held his hand, but sleep was elusive.

Lying there Cheron practiced deep breathing in an attempt to find equilibrium. Her thoughts, however, found no peace, frantically searching across the synapses for sources of comfort. Just before dawn, she arose and went to her small library of counseling texts and inspirational books, hoping for some words to begin filling the enormous void. Her sensation was of a chasm in the middle of her chest where her lungs should be, right beside a heart that was so stressed it literally ached as it pulsed. She was drawn to *Loneliness and Love* by Clark Moustakas. She was desperate for some words of encouragement to allow movement forward and out of the abyss of intense loneliness and loss.

And there it was, a passage she had highlighted last November when preparing to lead Uncle Alex's memorial service. It was as though the recent loss of her brother was preparation for facing what lay ahead. Moustakas wrote:

All love leads to suffering. If we did not care for others in a deep and fundamental way, we would not experience grief when they are troubled or disturbed, when they face tragedy or misfortune, when they are ill and dying. Every person is ultimately confronted with the pain of separation or death, with tragic grief that can be healed only in silence and isolation. When pain is accepted and felt as one's own, at the center of being, then suffering grows into compassion for other human beings and all living creatures. Through pain, the heart opens and out of sorrow come new sensations of levity and joy.

    She took the book and her Bible outside on the front stoop where she sat in her bathrobe and slippers as the sun rose and its rays came streaming through the trees. The warm summer morning was silent and peaceful as she read more passages to feed her hungry and wounded soul. There was strength and assurance in the Book of Psalms. The words and melody from the hymn, "Spirit of God, Descend Upon My Heart," kept cycling through her consciousness: "Teach me to feel that Thou art always nigh; Teach me the struggles of the soul to bear...Teach me the patience of unanswered prayer." She prayed that God would ease this pain and sorrow, open her heart, and help her figure out how there would ever be happiness and joy again without Scotty.
    Uncle Alex told me how, a short time later, Dad woke up and found Mom out front. They hugged and cried together in the yard. When they began to notice the birds chirping and the puppy barking for her breakfast, they inventoried the tasks that lay before them and decided on a division of labor. First they'd check on Phillip, then Mom would start making phone calls to family and friends while Dad contacted John, Dr. Chester, to figure out funeral arrangements. Before they were dressed, Phillip started vomiting and had to be rushed to the hospital in town and the phone started ringing with calls from neighbors and friends who wanted to help. Edna and Larry came from next door to answer the phone and to

be there for anyone who came by our house.

Phillip's concussion was causing his vomiting. The hospital kept him only an hour until it subsided and his tests came back okay. When he was home again in his own bed, sedated and resting peacefully, Gramma Edna said she'd take care of him while my parents went to the funeral parlor where my body had been moved. The funeral director was very helpful. The burial services were set, a small blue coffin was chosen, and they all drove up and over the crest of a hill at City View Cemetery to select a gravesite.

A doe grazing with her twin spotted fawns meandered away as they drove to a spot on a slope overlooking the Willamette River and facing west in the direction of our house, west of Salem. It was a lovely place and the decision was not hard, though shock and numbness had set in so that pondering options seemed unimportant or impossible. A young sapling grew very near the gravesite, its branches spreading a small patch of cooling shadow over the group. My grieving parents nodded to one another as they parted, agreeing that the placid deer family and the view toward home were good reasons to choose this final resting place for their dear child. Mom took the car and headed home to be with Phillip and to select burial clothes and shoes for me. The funeral director drove Dad to his office where they could finalize the arrangements.

When Dad arrived home an hour later, Mom had called to share the news with her oldest sister, Alice, in Seattle. The conversation was tearful, both sisters hardly over the loss of their only brother, his death and funeral just nine months earlier. When Mom heard Auntie Alice's voice on the phone, she said, "We've lost Scotty. Last evening he was killed in a car accident." Alice later told Mom that her brain got stuck on "lost" and refused to process the second sentence. She replied, "You're kidding," thinking that "lost" meant I'd wandered away and couldn't be found. It took some concentration to fathom the true message in its awful finality, and she was embarrassed that her response came out sounding so trivial.

Alice was the oldest of four sisters, and now the oldest child in the family since Uncle Alex's death. She had always been a "take-charge" kind of person and Mom was the same. Uncle Alex wasn't surprised as he observed how both my parents moved forward with the sad activities needing to be done. They were good at taking care of business and getting things done efficiently. It would take Dad's parents a day or two to fly from Texas, but he didn't see any reason to delay the burial and memorial service any longer than that. Mom was confident that Alice and her husband would assume the task of contacting all the other Seattle family members so they could plan their travel if they wanted to attend the memorial service on Monday.

Mom's best friend from college, Satsuki, called as soon as she heard news of the crash reported on the radio. Her youngest son was my friend at Little Beavers Preschool, and her other child was a boy about ten. The two moms had shared their experiences of raising two boys while going to graduate school full time. Now they cried together on the phone because one of the four boys – me – was killed on the highway. Satsuki jumped in her car and came straight to our house. She helped Mom to think clearly and quickly about a memorial so that money could be spent on something permanent instead of flowers that wilt and die right away.

Unk looked up abruptly from his view of activities on Earth when he heard me calling his name and pedaling confidently toward him.

"I'm back, Unk," I announced. I'd seen a few things during my spin around Heaven that I wanted to talk about, but first I wanted to know how things were going down in Oregon. Alex told me Phillip was home and resting. Mom and Dad were busy calling friends and family and making plans for the funeral.

"Boy, I bet everyone's missing me a lot. Let me look." I saw Mom was talking on the phone with the Easts. They owned the Little

Beavers Preschool and Daycare program where Phillip and I spent our days while Mom was nearby at college in Corvallis. Dad got on the extension phone line and the four of them worked out an agreement to create a memorial playground. That was the idea Satsuki and Mom had come up with. This information would be printed in the newspaper with the notice of my death, so people who loved and missed me could donate money. I thought that was a really cool idea. All my friends would be happy on new playground equipment and the school needed it. Before they hung up, the Easts asked if all the teachers could visit Phillip the next day, Sunday. Darn, that was the first time they ever went to our house, and I was disappointed because I wouldn't be there to show them my room, Heidi, and the treehouse out back.

Dad called Grandmother and Granddaddy in Austin. We hadn't seen them since September when we had gone to Texas for their fiftieth wedding anniversary party. That was a happy time. Then Phillip and I started preschool and Mom went back to college, which was fun, but Uncle Alex died in October and everyone was sad. Now everyone was very sad again. My grandparents were old and it wasn't easy for them to travel, but I knew they'd want to be close to help my parents. Grandmother reminded Daddy that she lost her first baby during childbirth and she knew how lonely and helpless it felt to lose a child. They would fly to Oregon on Sunday.

Phillip and I had godparents who lived in New York. They didn't have any kids yet but Sue loved to spoil me and feed me all the chocolate ice cream I could eat. Art loved to talk about basketball and football with Phillip. Phillip jabbered all the time about sports. Art said he sounded like Howard Cosell, the TV commentator. When my Dad called to tell them I died on Friday night, Sue promised she'd be on the next plane for Portland. Shoot! I knew Phillip was going to get the chocolate ice cream and I wouldn't even be there! Uncle Alex told me I'd get to eat anything I wanted in Heaven, but I was still upset about missing Sue, as well as all the teachers from Little Beavers.

Daddy called our friends all over the country; Phillip wet the bed and started crying so Mom helped him get a warm bath. People kept calling our house. Some from church and the neighborhood brought food. Good thing we had an extra freezer in the basement because there was a lot of food! It just kept coming. Heidi barked a greeting to anyone coming to the door, but people talked in hushed tones and didn't stay at the house or on the phone very long. This went on all afternoon and early evening until Sue called from the airport so Dad was happy to get away for a quiet drive to pick her up in Portland.

Mom had been thinking a lot about the memorial service at the church Monday afternoon. Now she had time to make phone calls. Pastor Ed was on a trip to the Holy Lands so she called a couple of other ministers who worshipped at our church. One was the father of a girl in my Sunday school class. He helped Mom through the arrangements. He said he could imagine how he'd feel if his daughter were killed, like me. Mom told him that many children would probably come to the service. He agreed that he would choose his words with that in mind. He also said he'd get an organist and some ushers.

Mom called the other pastor to ask if his son, Larry, would sing some selections recorded by Neil Diamond. Larry was a teenager who played guitar and sang in our church from time to time. He had a great voice for that kind of music, which Mom thought was "young" music. At least, modern kids and their parents all seemed to like Neil. He was one of the singers our family sang along with on the car radio when we were on road trips. I loved "Song Sung Blue" and "Sweet Caroline." Mom liked the music from the movie about Jonathan Livingston Seagull. Larry agreed he'd sing and play for the memorial service.

When Daddy and Sue arrived from the airport, the three of them all hugged and cried a lot. Phillip woke up and came to the family room where he got to be kissed and rocked by Sue. They nibbled on one of the casseroles a neighbor had brought, but nobody was hungry. They talked quietly, glad all the visitors were gone and the phone wasn't ringing anymore. Phillip fell asleep snuggled up against the dog on the floor.

Twenty-four hours had passed since I died and everyone in the family was exhausted. For the first time ever, Heidi was allowed to break the rules of her obedience training so she could sleep on Phillip's bed. I had tried a few times to sneak her in to sleep with me in my room, but she wouldn't break the rules. Tonight was different; she seemed to understand Phillip needed her. She curled up at his feet. Sue slipped beneath the covers on my bed in the next room and cried herself to sleep.

I wished I could tell Phillip about meeting up with Uncle Alex. He would have been jealous of all the fun I was having. I worried about him because he was bruised and scraped from the car wreck. He felt sleepy all the time from the pain medicines. Mom and Dad had told him that I died and wouldn't be around anymore but I don't think he understood. I figured maybe he'd get to thinking about Unk's dying, and how he was really gone forever after the cancer finally made him too skinny and weak to get out of bed. Phillip was also upset because I didn't have a seatbelt on when we crashed. He was thinking he should have buckled me in and kept me from dying. I knew it wasn't his fault. I wished I could tell him that, too.

3   Day Two, Sunday Morning

The phone started ringing early on Sunday, even before Heidi woke up and barked to be let outside. Phillip felt better and laughed a little as the dog nipped at the leg of his pajamas. A friend from the church called Mom for advice on what should be announced from the pulpit during the morning worship. Mom told her of the plans that had been made and that families should not be afraid to bring their little children, my friends, to the memorial service. The speeches and music and prayers weren't going to be too sad and scary. Besides our neighborhood and church friends, the families from Little Beavers were planning to come up from Corvallis.

When Mom hung up the phone, she remembered that the Little Beavers teachers were going to visit Phillip that afternoon. She helped him dress in some clean clothes but asked him to stay in bed or lie on the couch most of the time so his brain would get well. Usually he would have wanted to watch football games on TV, but I think he'd forgotten it was Sunday.

"Phillip," my mom reminded him, "your teachers are going to be here soon. And, the Boyds want you to stay over tonight at their house at the cherry orchard. Is that okay? They'll bring you to the church after lunch tomorrow for Scotty's memorial service. In a few hours Auntie Alice and her family will be here, and they're bringing Granny from Seattle. Auntie Mary and Auntie Connie will be coming too. You try to rest now before the house fills up with people."

Dad felt he needed to see a couple of his surgical patients in the hospital. He would drop off my burial clothes at the mortuary while he was in town. Dr. Boyd and Dr. Chester had told Dad they'd do his hospital work, but he felt it would be better to take care of that responsibility himself. That's the way my Dad operated; he didn't want his patients to feel he wasn't paying attention to them. Sometimes on Saturday mornings Dad would take Phillip and me to the hospital when he made rounds. The nurses loved to see us and always gave us treats, or maybe we'd get cinnamon rolls in the cafeteria. If a patient was doing okay, Dad sometimes introduced us. Most of the time the sick people would smile and be happier. I got a lot of good ideas that I used when I played emergency paramedic or "Dr. Mayhall" with my school friends.

Mom had remembered more old friends she wanted to call so they wouldn't be "the last to know" the news of my death. Mostly these were college friends who still lived in Oregon. She talked with a couple in Portland and they agreed to spread the word.

Mom's sorority sister, Anne, whose family we had visited a month earlier on a trip to Tacoma, was stunned and immediately offered to send money for the playground memorial. Everyone my parents talked with seemed to like the idea and the checks started pouring in the next week.

Finally Mom called a college friend who lived in New Hampshire. They talked for over ten minutes. They had been very close during student years and the bond was still strong though they were living on two different sides of the country. All this sharing and support seemed to lift Mom's spirits, and Sue was taking a little nap, so I felt okay about getting back to Uncle Alex and my exploration of Heaven.

4   Heavenly Home

"So, Unk, where do you live here in Heaven?" I asked.

"C'mon," he replied, "I can show you and introduce you to some friends of yours you've yet to meet. They have been watching over your family for a long time. Now they are looking forward to having you near."

I mounted my bike again but I didn't have to pedal slowly because Uncle Alex's legs were very long and he walked fast. It looked like his knobby, crooked knees which had caused him so much pain were straight and strong now. I was pretty sure he could run if I speeded up. Since I wasn't sure where we were headed, I let him set our pace. We passed through what looked like a regular neighborhood on Earth with an assortment of houses and trees, but there were no cars, trucks, buses or trains in sight. I didn't see any spaceships or launch pads either, like they had down at Cape Canaveral in Florida.

When I had taken my earlier bike ride around Heaven, I hadn't gone very far. I saw some other angel-people but I avoided them and pedaled by quickly because they were strangers, and because I'm sort of shy. I was happy to see that this place wasn't ugly or weird. The sky was blue and the grass was green, just like Oregon. The air didn't look brown and breathing was easy. I remembered how upset Mom had been, on our trips to visit our family in Seattle, because of the brown air. "The air was always clean and fresh when I was growing up here," she told us. Whenever I saw brown air covering Seattle I tried to remember not to breathe too much until we got out of it.

As Uncle Alex and I moved along through the heavenly neighborhood, I asked him where I'd find babies or little kids my age. I was remembering the talk about Heaven and Bible stories I'd heard in Sunday school. "Hey, is Baby Jesus here, or Moses in the Bulrushes? Does Jesus have any lambs?"

"Sure," Unk chuckled, "Jesus lives here, but he's grown up and I haven't seen him recently because his house isn't in this part of Heaven. I don't think he has lambs now. And Moses sure isn't a bulrushes baby anymore! I understand he lives in a retirement village, but I haven't been there yet. The old people I have spent the most time with are Grandma Strom, your great-grandmother who died when your mom was in college, and one of your mom's high school teachers who lives next door to us. I live in the same big house with Grandma. She has been taking in some of the little ones who have been coming to Heaven since the 1960's. There are lots of children under our roof. You'll see, it's a great place." He grinned, "I think you'll have as much fun playing with them as I do."

He slowed his pace outside a large, two-story frame house with a huge wrap-around porch and a beautiful yard. I heard the screen door slam and glanced over to see a lady who looked very much like my mom, only older. She wore a full apron of fabric covered in tiny flowers and trimmed in green. Her gray hair was combed back in a bun, but it was still soft around her face. I figured it must be Grandma Strom, but thought I'd better check before I got too excited.

"She looks like Mom," I told Uncle Alex. He explained that people had been saying that for years. Evidently my mother, Cheron, was the "spitting image" of this great-grandma person when they were both kids. Unk reminded me of the gilt-framed picture that hung over the piano in the living room at my Seattle Granny's house. It showed this great-grandma as a child of four, taken about 1900. For sure, this woman still looked like that black-and-white portrait, and she looked like my mom, too.

As she reached down to pick me up, a bunch of other children came out of the house and the back yard. I was glad to see that my heaven would have people of all ages, not just grown-ups. She carried me to a perch on the railing surrounding the porch. Most of the kids gathered around, except for four who crawled into Uncle Alex's large lap when he sat down on the porch swing.

"Well, well," said the lady who looked like my mom, only older. "We are so delighted to welcome you, Scotty, and hope you will choose to stay in our home. We have prepared a special place for you upstairs. Do you want a room of your own, or would you like one of the other boys to share space with you?"

I had to think a minute about that. At home in Oregon I liked having my own room where Phillip wouldn't mess with my stuff. But, right then, I thought it might be nice to have a best friend my age nearby. A small, blonde-haired boy with huge brown eyes tugged at my leg. He said he liked my cowboy boots and he begged me to be his roommate. "Okay," I said, "but I hope you have toys. I don't seem to have any of my stuff here. Hey, what's your name?" The boy beamed and looked proudly at great-grandma and the other kids.

"My name's Steve," he answered. "Your uncle has become an uncle to all of us here, and GG is the boss of our home. She makes the rules and she cooks all the food." He went on to point out, one by one, Lila, Esther, Sasha, Freddy, Gilberto, Nathan, Osmin, Samuel, Heather and Jesus. The last four were swinging with Unk, and the rest were trying to get close enough to touch me. Most of them didn't have shoes on and they were curious about my brown, scuffed-up boots with the holes in the toes. Freddy wanted to grab my equipment from my belt, but I moved his hand away just in time. I never liked strangers messing with my stuff.

I thought back to my days at Little Beavers when I got put in time-out for being selfish with my equipment. One time I was so bothered by another kid I hit him and tore up his art papers. And once I knocked over a girl's block tower because she took my ropes out of my cubby. I needed to protect all my gear. I was afraid the other kids would lose it or break it. I could see that I'd have to be more patient here in Heaven because I'd arrived with only a few toys. Steve had nodded when I asked him about his toys. I could hardly wait to see what he had upstairs. I was hoping for lots of books, puzzles and Legos.

"You should call me GG," the boss lady said. "I am your great-grandmother, but you already have grandmas on Earth and it might be easier to abbreviate my name. Is that okay? Everyone in these parts knows me as GG." She went on to tell me about my mom when she was a little girl and went to stay with GG at the farm. I learned that GG and her husband had chickens in the back and a small, cement-enclosed irrigation ditch running across the front yard. All the kids gathered around GG to hear the tales of her life on Earth. I knew that Uncle Alex was famous as a storyteller, but it appeared that my GG was good at it, too.

"I especially remember the time when your mom was four, just about your age. The doctor had had some problems getting her tonsils out and she was very sick. Since her mother was working and the other kids were in school, Cheron came from Seattle to Wapato to recuperate with us. After a few days of pampering with lots of ice cream and Jell-O, she regained her energy and her voice. Pretty soon she was out back cackling at the hens, spreading their grain on the ground and carefully gathering the eggs from the nests. She loved to help in the kitchen, especially breaking open the eggs. We baked dozens of cookies for her to take back and share with the other kids in Seattle.

"We had to keep an eye on your mom because she was fascinated watching the water bugs in the irrigation ditch," GG continued. "Once when she bent with her pail to catch bugs she fell in head first and the current pulled at her. She screamed her head off and we arrived in time to rescue her. The water wasn't deep and there was little chance of her drowning, but she was sopping wet and scared, so I let her stay a little afraid and she never gave us that kind of trouble again."

"Do you have chickens and water bugs here?" I asked.

"No, but there are a couple of honking geese that strut around the back yard. That reminds me," GG said with a hearty laugh, "a goose we had back in Wapato used to chase your mother when she was little. One Sunday she was dressed and ready for church. She headed for grandpa's car out back and Gertie the Goose started after her. She ran and hollered, but by the time I got out there Gertie had her cornered and was plucking all the bright buttons off her coat. Cheron tried to kick the goose and make it go away, but Gertie was persistent and didn't stop until all but one of the buttons was on the ground. It was hard not to laugh, but your mom was so distressed and tearful. Thankfully, Gertie didn't swallow any of the metal buttons and we were able to get them all sewn back on the coat and still get to Sunday school on time."

All the children laughed, and it was obvious they loved GG's stories. I was beginning to look forward to life in this happy house with Unk, GG and so many kids my age. "Can we go inside now?" I asked. I had never lived in a house with a real upstairs, only ones with daylight basements. Uncle Alex stood up with Osmin and Jesus in his arms, while Heather and Samuel each clung to one of his legs. There was a rush to get through the door all at once, until GG said, "Line up, darlings," and each child appeared to know his place in the new order. She took me by the hand and we went to the front so we could enter first.

The house was huge. I had always thought my giant uncle needed a bigger house than he had on Earth, and now he was living in one!

It was so large and there was so much going on with all the kids that I decided I would explore later when things quieted down. A big chart that was mounted on the dining room wall near the kitchen door caught my eye. I did a double-take when I realized that I could READ all the words on it! I saw all the children's names listed and I read them out loud: "Esther, Freddy, Gilberto, Heather, Jesus, Lila, Nathan, Osmin, Samuel, Sasha, Scotty and Steve." In a repeated order beside the names there were three chores listed: "Feed the geese, dust all the furniture down low, put away the clean silverware."

"I can read!" I screamed in surprise. "I always wanted to read, like Phillip read when he was four, but I just couldn't figure it out when I was on Earth, except I could read the nametags of all my school friends...Missy, Adrian, Brenton, Justin and Jarrett. Oh, GG, this is the most wonderful magic! Thank you. Unk, did you hear me reading?"

Uncle Alex and all the kids were laughing, but he managed to answer. "Scotty, we knew you'd really like this surprise. It's one of Heaven's blessings. You know, I was not a good reader. School was very hard for me because of it. I could never sound out the words easily, as you just did. We didn't have many books in our home, and my mom – your Seattle grandma – needed to work so much that she didn't have time to read to us. It took me a long time to finish all the classes and graduate from high school.

"Lucky for me, I could tell good stories and jokes, I loved to sing in the choirs at school and church, and I was a very good basketball player and golfer. Some teachers didn't enjoy having me in their classes because I was a class clown. But I had many friends and teammates. I was president of the choir. The coaches – especially the high school basketball coach – were like fathers to me. Coach Means wanted me to be the center on his team, so he helped me get a tutor for the reading and writing that was required. Your Auntie Alice and I were in some of the same classes so she helped me sometimes, too.

"Imagine how happy I was when I got to Heaven and it all came so easily. Why, one of my favorite pastimes is settling into that big armchair in the living room and reading stories as this gaggle of children gathers around. Of course, they can all read their own books, if they want to, but reading and talking about the pictures together is a dandy way to spend an evening."

I felt a twinge of sadness remembering story time with my mom or dad and Phillip, and story circle with my teacher, Rhonda, at Little Beavers. I was going to miss a lot of things now that I was in Heaven forever, but at least reading and books were popular in GG's house.

My chest puffed up with pride as I looked over at the chart again. "Hey, Unk, I thought you said that Jesus lived in another part of Heaven. Isn't that his name in the middle of the list?"

Everyone started laughing again. "I guess you never had a friend on Earth named 'Hay-zeus'," explained GG, "but that name is common here and in many countries of the world. This is our Jesus," she said, as a little black-haired boy scrambled out of the crowd. "The Jesus you're thinking of is the special Son of God that you learned about in Sunday school. He does live a good distance away from here. From time to time we pack a big picnic lunch and head over to the lakeside where he tells stories. Last time we went he asked Uncle Alex to lead the singing. The crowd there is always joyful and Alex chooses familiar songs and hymns that make people want to dance and laugh."

This certainly did appear to be a place where joy and happiness were constant. It wasn't anything like the outer space I'd seen on TV. Here we were, up above the Earth, just as Captain Commander James Kirk and the crew of Starship Enterprise flew on their missions. But there didn't seem to be anything to fear here, as far as I could tell. It was beautiful and all the people I had met were kind and loving toward me. I thought for a moment that I might like to see Dr. Helena Russell, Barbara Bain's character, who was always helping people and aliens on the show, "Space 1999."

But, for now, I was getting hungry for some of GG's cooking. I was hoping the other kids wouldn't think I was a baby if I needed a nap. All this activity in Heaven was wearing me out! Boy, was I relieved to hear GG say that we'd be having toasted cheese sandwiches shortly, then all the children would find comfy spots on the floor or furniture in the living room where they could get a midday rest.

5 Day Two, Sunday p.m.

At our house in Oregon a parade of family and friends arrived on that Sunday, one day before my funeral and memorial service. First came two carloads of teachers from Little Beavers. My teacher, Rhonda, was trying to smile, but the tears just kept coming. The Easts, who owned the preschool, each took one of Phillip's hands as he sat up in his bed, resting on fluffed pillows. He looked and acted like the pictures in our book of nursery rhymes, Old King Cole in his counting house calling for his pipe and his fiddlers three. Phillip got very excited as seven teachers encircled his bed, filling the room. The teachers had brought some gifts of books and toys. One of them sat down on the bed to read aloud a story Phillip's class had written and illustrated together a couple weeks earlier. It was about their field trip to the farm petting zoo. Phillip couldn't stop giggling as he remembered the comments of his classmates and saw the funny drawings they'd made on the pages. The teachers left after about thirty minutes with promises to see Phillip again on Monday at the memorial service.

Just after noon, the aunts, uncles, cousins and my granny drove their three cars into the driveway. Most came from Seattle, five hours away. The grown-ups got out of the cars and stretched while the kids started running around our yard as soon as the car doors swung open. The kids were shushed but it didn't quiet them much. Mom came out of the house to greet them. All the women did a lot of hugging while the two uncles tried to corral my wild cousins. Eight or ten children from this family could really cause a ruckus with their chasing and hollering.

My godmother, Sue, had lemonade and cookies ready. She invited the grown-ups indoors to get refreshments, but she offered a tray of drinks in paper cups to the children who continued to race around the front yard. A couple of them were hanging upside down on the swing set. My twin cousins, David and Danny, were playing a keep-away game with Heidi as she barked and wiggled in delight. Inside the house, the parents discussed and decided who would be able to fit into our house for a sleepover. Dad suggested some motels in downtown Salem where they could get reservations for the people who were left over.

Auntie Connie asked questions about the events planned for the next day. Mom seemed upset that she hadn't had time to think about what she'd wear. Connie was my youngest aunt and she wasn't married and didn't have any children. She put an arm around Mom and told her they'd go on a shopping trip into town to find just the right dress for a sunny summer day – a dress that "Scotty would have liked" and one that would make Mom feel pretty and not so sad. While the families with kids coaxed Phillip to come out of his bedroom to visit or play, Mom and Auntie Connie hopped into the car and headed for the mall.

"Even though black or navy blue is traditional for funerals, you really should wear a dress that makes people remember Scotty with happiness," suggested Connie. They went to a fancier department store where Mom never shopped because she didn't like to spend so much money. She almost never bought us clothes that weren't on sale because she felt the TV ads usually made kids want things that were overpriced. I had lots of hand-me-downs from Phillip and some from Auntie Alice's boys: David, Daniel and Darren Kelly. I loved it when I grew into the big boys' clothes. Relatives usually gave us special new outfits on our birthdays and Christmas. Auntie Connie wanted Mom to have a lovely, new dress. They settled for one with lime-colored flowers on a white background, with ruffles around the scooped neckline and a skirt that touched the floor.

Mom read the label out loud, "Size 10, and washable." She was pleased to fit easily into the size ten. My aunt complimented her on her figure as she zipped the summery dress up the back, with ease. The figure she saw in the mirror lifted some of the gloominess Mom was feeling and she managed a smile and a thank-you. "You were quite a bit heavier last Christmas, right?" asked Auntie Connie. "How did you lose all the weight?"

Mom reflected on her weight gain in the months following Uncle Alex's death. She told Connie that she tended to overeat when stressed, and that was the period when she had started her doctoral studies, too. Every weekday morning Mom, Phillip and I left home early in the little car for the thirty-mile drive to Corvallis where we got dropped off at Little Beavers and Mom continued on to Oregon State. We ate or finished our breakfast on the road and got in the habit of eating most of the time when we were in the car, both coming and going. Besides the driving, Mom was in classes or doing homework for many hours every day and she got very little physical exercise. The pounds began to stick and she had to buy some bigger clothes, which made her mad.

"Don't get me wrong, Connie," Mom went on. "We had some happy times during that fall and winter of 1976-77, and I loved the stimulation of being back in college. Little Beavers was a wonderful environment for Phillip and Scotty. I made many new friends with other graduate students and the faculty. In fact, I got so involved with all that was new in my life that I neglected my relationship with Bill. I went on my merry way every day, taking the boys with me and spending long days, and sometimes evenings for night classes, down in Corvallis. Bill was working about eighty hours a week building his medical practice. We spent few waking hours together. I didn't realize we were in trouble until spring when we began to quarrel and I avoided the potential pain of discussions.

"Finally he blasted me with angry words one Sunday and I faced the reality that I needed to change some things, quick. We planned our schedules so we spent more time together both with and without the boys. Our relationship started to improve. That was when I also realized I was thirty pounds overweight and hating myself for it. So I signed up for a tennis class during summer session at OSU and made good progress with diet and exercise. We were having a great summer and I was feeling much better about our marriage and family life until now, this horrible accident...Scotty dying." She sat down in the tiny dressing room and sobbed, then suddenly realized she needed to change out of the new dress so she wouldn't soil it with tears and a runny nose.

    It pleased Auntie Connie to buy this special dress for Mom. They paid the cashier, then hurried from the mall to stop by the grocery store for some beverages. Friends had brought plenty of food to provide supper for the fifteen adults and children who had gathered at the house. My dad ate hurriedly, then invited David and Danny to drive with him to the airport to pick up my grandparents from Texas. When the dishes were washed people sat about the family room trying to make small talk that wouldn't start them crying. Mom remembered the final viewing was scheduled at the funeral parlor and invited her sisters to go with her to see me for the last time.

    Soft music played as they entered the room where my body lay in the small, blue casket. The four women felt almost unbearable sadness and grief. Only two days earlier I had been playing and working and sleeping and eating just like everyone else. Now my body was lying perfectly still in a frilly box, but my angel-spirit was alive and well, viewing it all from my heavenly home. Weird.

    Mom caressed my face and my stiff body, which was dressed in the red and green plaid jacket I had worn for Easter and my birthday in March. It was a hand-me-down from Auntie Alice's youngest boy. Phillip had a jacket to match which had belonged to one of the twins. We looked like grown-ups when we dressed in them for Sunday school.

"Our whole family is crazy about plaids," Uncle Alex explained to me. "GG was from the Scottish family or clan called MacGregor. Her brother was the drum major for the Seattle Police bagpipe band and we were so proud when he marched by in the Seafair and Santa Claus parades every year. Not everyone enjoys the squealing music of bagpipes, but that was usually what we anticipated most as we sat on the curb along the parade route down Fifth Avenue."

Finally Mom brushed aside the blonde hair on my forehead and remarked to her sisters, "Scotty's bangs were just now growing out after he and a school friend whacked them off a few months ago. I was so angry with him because I had made an appointment for the boys to have their joint birthday photograph. I yelled at him before I regained my composure and saw the humor in it. We went ahead with the photos and they came out cute, even though he was scalped in the front!"

My body's feet were wearing shiny black shoes I'd never seen before. Mom started crying as she touched them, explaining, "I bought these shoes for him on sale, figuring he'd grow into them by Christmas. They're too big, but he'll never have a chance to grow into them now." The tears rolled down her cheeks. She had also chosen a small stuffed-animal rabbit from my Easter basket and my tattered blankie to tuck into the coffin beside me. Auntie Alice stepped forward and touched my cold, stiff hand, but had to turn away as she started sobbing uncontrollably.

Mom reached up like a stiff robot to shut the coffin lid, aching for some way to end this painful moment. Auntie Alice reached over and took both her hands away. "Leave it, Cheron," she said. Then all the sisters joined arms, supporting one another to the car, and headed back to our house.

My grandmother and granddaddy from Texas had arrived. They usually had presents for Phillip and me when they came to visit, but not this time. My grandmother was a famous writer of Indian stories and she liked to bring us books. She knew all about cowboys and Indians. Her house in Austin was filled with beautiful rugs, pots and baskets the Indians had made. She told us stories about the Old West and I loved to dress up like the wranglers pictured in some of the books.

My mom and dad had inherited several pieces of the grandparents' Indian artwork and later purchased some of their own from trading posts around New Mexico, where we lived when I was a baby. Our house in Salem was decorated Western-style, too, mixing American Indian and cowboy stuff with souvenirs Mom had gathered when she worked with Indians in Honduras during her Peace Corps years. We had beaded moccasins, Navajo rugs, a huge tom-tom, Kachina dolls, and a cool tomahawk in the display case in the living room.

Once for summer vacation our family met up with Art and Sue from New York and went to a dude ranch in Montana. The ranch had horses and cows and rabbits all over the place, and a big St. Bernard mascot. That's where I really learned to be a cowboy, and where we got the idea of getting our Heidi-pie. That's what Daddy liked to call her – "Heidi-pie."

Heidi now rested her big head in Granddaddy's lap, which seemed to console him a little. My grandmother Mildred was trying to help Daddy pack some clothes for Phillip who was going to sleep over at Dr. Boyd's house. Judy and Hal Boyd had a little boy my age. We had celebrated our fourth birthdays together with lots of kids at their house. They owned a cherry orchard and I remembered what fun we'd had playing hide-and-seek under millions of blossoming trees. Some of the kids at the party ran around and yelled a lot, but I knew how to play the game quietly and it took a long time for the person who was "it" to find my hiding place. At that moment, I kind of wished I could yell real loud to the folks below to tell them I was doing okay in Heaven, but Unk had told me that wouldn't be possible.

When Phillip left with the Boyds that night, my aunties and uncles gathered up all my wild cousins and they went to a motel downtown to spend the night, settling on a plan to meet at the mortuary in the morning. Just the three grandparents and Sue stayed to sleep in the empty beds at our house. Everyone was very tired and gloomy.

Granddaddy asked, "What can I do to help?" My mom, Cheron, loved the old guy, even though he was often very stern and judgmental. She remembered when Daddy first introduced her to his parents in 1967. Granddaddy quizzed her to see if she was smart. When she told him about her hopes and dreams for her life and the world, he scoffed and said, "You must be stupid!" He wasn't used to such idealism and optimism, being a pessimist at heart. Now he was feeling very kindly and tender toward his only daughter-in-law, desperate to do something – anything – that might help ease the pain.

"Well, Temple," Mom said, "I'm thinking you might build us a memory box to store some of Scotty's most precious things." Granddaddy was an architect and a school administrator, but he was a master woodworker as well. "I just want a small box for his special toys and treasures. As a teenager, I babysat for a boy with spina bifida. When that little boy died his parents couldn't bring themselves to change anything but instead made a shrine out of his bedroom. That felt morbid and impractical to me. I saw how the mother never seemed to get over her grief and go on with her life." They settled on a cube-shaped box measuring fifteen inches in all directions. Granddaddy seemed relieved that he'd have something meaningful to contribute.

As they planned to retire for the night, Mom apologized that the sheets were not clean on my bed and Phillip's. She was grateful and surprised when Sue said she'd done the wash and changed all the beds. New towels were hung in both bathrooms. My Seattle grandma, who was much younger than the ones from Texas, volunteered to sleep on the couch so Temple and Mildred could each have a kid bed. Sue had made herself a pallet on the floor next to Mom's side of my parents' bed, wanting to stay very close and be helpful if they needed her during the night. Sue was a nurse. She knew how to take good care of people who were hurting. Everyone in our house that night was missing me and hurting a lot.

6 The Funeral

Uncle Alex helped GG tuck the other kids into their beds, then sat and swung me in the porch swing as we watched all that happened in Salem on the day of my funeral. Unk said he wanted to keep watch over his family. I begged to watch with him.

The Earth-day started out when Auntie Alice drove back to our house at 7 a.m. She had not been able to sleep at the motel, so she quietly laid out all the clothes she planned for her three sons to wear and asked Uncle Maynard to see they were dressed and had breakfast at a nearby Denny's restaurant. Then they could walk to meet the family at the funeral home by ten o'clock. She tiptoed over the boys sleeping on the floor, quietly escaping to the car and drove to our house.

Mom woke up very early, too. She couldn't get back to sleep. They made a pot of coffee and talked about the funeral and memorial. Mom remarked, with regret, "I may have made a mistake telling everyone in the obituary notice not to send flowers but to contribute to the playground fund instead. What if there aren't any flowers at all in the church?"

"If I remember right," replied Auntie Alice, "Scotty loved to gather wildflower bouquets for you. Why don't we walk around the yard and down the road to see what's blooming now? That may be more appropriate than florist flowers anyhow." It was mid-summer and all the spring flowers had long-since faded, but they found some blue and purple bachelor buttons and a few roses in the yard. Along the roadway they spied some additional wild roses in pale pink, and white daisies. To these they added an armload of foliage and weeds in many shades of green. It was beautiful and made Mom smile. They stuck all they'd gathered in a big tub of water before going inside to wake the others and dress for the funeral. Sue from New York and my Texas grandparents were wide awake because they came from different time zones and hadn't adjusted yet.

Uncle Alex's wife, Auntie Ginny, arrived from Seattle with her three kids. She had decided not to come the day before because she felt overwhelmed with grief, first for Unk and now for me. She figured a one-day trip, back and forth, was about all she could stand. She had to get the kids up about 5 a.m. to drive the distance by ten o'clock. They were a bit late; my parents, grandparents and Sue were already loading themselves into our Volkswagen van for the trip to the mortuary. After another round of hugs and tears in the driveway, Auntie Ginny followed the van in her car so they could meet the rest of the Seattle family in town. Auntie Alice's car brought up the rear.

Only my family members were invited to the burial. My great-uncle Bill and great-aunt Peggy showed up unexpectedly, bringing a beautiful wreath of white rosebuds and daisies. They lived just 40 miles away and had read about the accident in their newspaper. Of course, Phillip got to sleep in and eat breakfast with the Boyd family at the cherry orchard, so he wasn't at the graveyard.

The sight of the little blue casket made everyone start crying again. That's why Mom and Dad had thought to keep the gathering small with just family, excluding Phillip, because he was still sick from the accident and not understanding all that had happened to him so quickly. I was glad to see Rev. McAmis, my church friend's dad. He said all the burying words and prayers. At least, that's what Unk told me. I had never been to a funeral so I didn't know what was supposed to happen, except they'd put the box with the body into the ground and pile a mound of dirt over it. Actually, they didn't bury the box until all the family left the cemetery. Mom had handed out little sprigs from the wildflower bouquet to everyone present. She led the way after the service, each person laying his or her flowers on the casket as they departed for the memorial service at the church.

Dad led the car caravan from the cemetery on the hill to the church parking lot downtown. When Mom got out of the car in her beautiful new dress, a tall man I didn't recognize approached her. Turns out it was her first boyfriend in college, David. He and his family lived in Forest Grove, outside of Portland. He was an administrator at Pacific University. That's where he and Mom went to college, and his wife went there, too. He shook Dad's hand and hugged my Mom. She thanked him for coming. He was early and agreed to wait outside to watch for other college friends who might show up. The rest of the family went inside to my Sunday school room to visit until the service started at one o'clock. It was a hot summer day so anyone wearing black clothes had started to sweat and feel uncomfortable in the bright sunshine.

While they were waiting, Dad started talking with Auntie Ginny about the bike trip our two families took in 1976, when Uncle Alex led the pack. Up in Heaven, we two swinging angels listened in and smiled with the remembering of good times on Earth. It was Unk who proposed to bike the whole length of the Oregon coast, which turned out to be 380 miles. He talked my parents into it. The two families planned to do it in one week, camping out by night and riding hard by day. Unk chose to start on the longest day of the year, in June, reasoning that would allow plenty of daylight hours to pedal.

Dad smiled as he remembered out loud, "Of course, we hadn't totally realized that June could still be very cold and rainy on the coast." The family, waiting for the start of the memorial service, listened with interest as the story unfolded. They were reminded of good times with Uncle Alex and the funny stories he could tell about adventures he'd dreamed up.

"Ginny, it was a good thing that you had been injured playing soccer and decided to drive the camper truck as a sag wagon," said Dad. "We might have drowned in rain or been washed into the Pacific Ocean on some of those seven days." Auntie Ginny and Unk's teenage daughter, Marti, were happy to babysit Phillip and me during the trip. We would all try to get up early each morning to wave good-bye to the bikers – Dad, Mom, Unk and Unk's youngest son, "crazy Andre" – as they set off for fifty or sixty miles of biking to the next campground where we had reservations.

"Do you remember," they laughed, "how Alex's long legs stuck way out to the sides as he pedaled because his bike was too small. You could see him coming or going a half mile away and know for sure it was him." They complained about the strain of the mountainous terrain and the foul weather that kept them drenched with rain and sweating at the same time. "My back and my butt were killing me," Dad continued, "and I could tell Alex was in horrible pain. But he was never a quitter, making jokes to help us forget our achy muscles and joints so we could forge on."

I remembered how Unk took a lot of pills when we were all together camping at night after a long day, four people riding and the rest of us driving the van, shopping and setting up the tent at our next stop. His knees and back were very sore, and he also complained of tummy aches. "Unk," I asked, "do your remember how much your stomach hurt on the bike trip? Was it the food Auntie Ginny cooked for us over the campfire or the junk food you bikers ate from pit-stop stores along the way?"

"Well, Scotty, I think I know now that my stomach pain was from the cancer starting, but we thought back then it was just indigestion. I took a lot of Tums, didn't I?"

The family members waiting for the start of the church service weren't talking about Unk's cancer and pain on my funeral day. They stuck to the funny stories from the bike trip. "We all had helmets with reflector strips and tall orange flags attached to our bikes so motorists would be able to see us," Dad's story continued. "The biggest challenge was keeping tabs on Andre who biked like a jackrabbit, racing ahead of the group in a powerful spurt of energy, then lurching to a stop when you least expected it. After about three days of worrying he'd get hit by a car any minute, I was checking the gears on his bike and discovered the kid's brakes were totally gone. No wonder he sped down the long hills like a maniac and was desperate to stop as soon as he slowed enough to hop off!"

Down there in my Sunday school room, Andre blushed bright red as my relatives laughed, all of them knowing how typical this was of his behavior. He tended to bounce around from one activity to another with little sense of where he was headed or how to get there. "I think he has learning disabilities like I did," said Uncle Alex of his youngest son, "and we'd hoped this challenging bike trip of seven days and a big goal at the end would help him learn patience and how to stick with a task."

"And we did it, didn't we, Unk? I remember the picture we took of all of us and the bikes in front of the sign saying, 'Welcome to California.' By the time we got to California the sun was shining every day. We were so happy that Auntie Ginny got a shop to make us matching tee-shirts with words saying, 'I Biked the Oregon Coast, 380 Miles, June 1976'." I hugged my big uncle when I looked up to see he was crying and smiling at the same time as he remembered those love-filled days on Earth. "I love you, Uncle Alex," I said, hoping he would stop being sad now that I was with him in Heaven.

7 *The Memorial Service*

It was almost one o'clock when Judy Boyd brought Phillip to the room where the family was waiting. "Sorry we're running late," she explained. "The parking lot is full and we had to park on the street three blocks away." Phillip looked much healthier after his sleepover with friends. He was dressed in his checkered "leisure" suit with a white turtleneck underneath, which made him look like a grown-up man, except short. Judy had parted his hair on the wrong side so he looked odd to me. No one else seemed to notice.

"Don't you look handsome," Auntie Ginny said, greeting him with a hug. He looked quickly around the packed room and said, "Where's Uncle Alex?" before he remembered that Unk wasn't part of these family gatherings anymore. Nobody had a chance to answer because right about then the usher came. He invited them to follow him down the side aisle to three long pews up front that were reserved for the family. Dad held Phillip's hand and Mom followed holding Granny's hand. Then came the old ones from Texas, and Sue, to fill up one whole pew.

As the rest of my relatives filed in, Mom checked out the beauty of the sanctuary and the organ music. Unk told me it was the prayer from the opera, "Hansel and Gretel." It was pretty, happy music, not depressing and sad. Mom was grateful Rev. McAmis had relayed her wishes to the organist. "Your Mom also requested that the organist play 'Leia's Theme from Star Wars,' the theme from the movie, 'Brian's Song,' and 'Song Sung Blue, Everybody Knows One'," Unk continued. "She wanted people to hear music that would remind them of you, and music that would touch their hearts with hope, not just sorrow."

Sunlight streamed in gold and purple rays through the stained-glass windows. The church ladies had decorated the front of the church with plenty of flowers. Friends and relatives from far away who couldn't come, or hadn't heard that they were supposed to send money for the playground fund at Little Beavers, had sent bouquets and wreaths. The church was beautiful and it was so packed that many people had to stand way in the back.

The minister prayed three times. He gave a little talk saying my name again and again and telling everyone that I was a good kid. He spoke especially to the parents and little children who had come, telling them that "Children aren't supposed to die...this was a bad accident...God makes everything suitable and beautiful in its time...there is a rhythm to life..." things like that. He read from the Bible about the seasons for getting born and dying, planting and picking the vegetables and flowers, crying and laughing, mending and sewing, loving and hating.

The best part was Larry's beautiful singing and guitar playing. You could hear his feelings in his voice as he sang the words about Jonathan Livingston Seagull. I remembered that Neil Diamond wrote and sang these songs, though these weren't my favorites when we sang along with Neil on the car radio. Phillip and I liked to chime in on the chorus of "Cracklin' Rose" or "Sweet Caroline." But for church, Jonathan's songs were better:

> Be, as a page that aches for a word which speaks on a theme that is timeless, while the sun god will make for your day.
>
> Sing, as a song in search of a voice that is silent, and the one God will make for your way.

The sun god and the One God seemed like they were right there in the church helping all the people and kids get used to my dying and becoming an angel living up here with God, Jesus, Uncle Alex and GG.

Mom, Dad, Phillip and the grandparents all lined up at the main door to hug people before they could leave, but some people tried to escape out the side doors of the church. Most of the adults were hanging their heads or crying into their handkerchiefs or Kleenex, but the children were smiling and chattering, unless they were shy like Patty from my Sunday school class. Patty almost never talked. She was hiding behind her mother after the funeral service. Mom noticed a fancy lady, dressed in a black suit and a hat with a net veil covering her face, as she tried to sneak out the back way. When Mom recognized that it was Lani and her husband, Ted, she left the greeters line to thank them for coming. These were friends from the days in New Mexico who had also moved to Oregon. They remembered me from the time I was a little baby. Lani clung to Mom as she sobbed; she felt so sad she could hardly talk.

Granddaddy couldn't get over the crowd. "Amazing that you've only lived in Salem for two years," he observed, "and already you have so many friends." It was true: Dad had tons of friends who were doctors and nurses in Salem; Mom had tons of other friends from Corvallis and Oregon State; Phillip and I had friends from Little Beavers and from preschools we'd attended in Salem, Montessori and the Lutheran Church daycare; and there were Mom's old college friends from Pacific University. Of course, hundreds of people from our church came. The doctor who took care of Phillip and me was there, even though he should have been in his office taking care of sick kids on a Monday afternoon. Mom cried the most when the big lady, Sally, who was her boss when she volunteered at the Teen Parent Program, hugged her. This lady had many grown children of her own. She was kind of like a grandma to all the babies who were born to the teenagers who were in the YWCA program. She loved to hold me in her lap when we went with Mom to the Y. Eunice, who always rocked me in the Sunday school nursery, was at the service, but she couldn't talk much because she just kept bawling.

My own grandma from Seattle – Phillip and I called her Granny – didn't say much the whole time she was in Salem. She had been a lot quieter in the months since her only son, Uncle Alex, had died in October. Mom had always been proud of Granny's history as a strong person and hard worker. She told us, "After your grandfather, Alex, Sr. died, she raised us five children as a single parent most of the time. Except when she tried out a second husband for a few years until he realized he couldn't handle living in a house with teenagers. When that husband left, Unk became 'the man of the house' and was in charge of helping raise four sisters: Auntie Alice, Auntie Mary, Me, and Auntie Connie."

Granny worked factory and waitress jobs, sometimes two or three jobs at the same time to support her kids. Mom said she was tough. She wasn't comfortable having people see her cry so she just didn't let herself do it in public. She was anxious to be on the road for Seattle soon after the memorial service so she could get back to her job building airplanes for Boeing. It worked out fine because all the Seattle relatives had to get back to their jobs, too.

They were already packed up from the motel and ready to roll. No one had eaten much since breakfast time, except that Auntie Mary had thought to stop at Safeway to buy some crackers and cheese for snacking while waiting at the church. The cousins traded their dress-up clothes for tee-shirts and shorts and piled into the cars headed for McDonald's, then on to Seattle.

8   A Heavenly Roommate

"That was a good funeral, wasn't it Unk?" I asked. " I liked the music and the flowers, but I was sorry that nobody played with the building blocks and puzzles in my Sunday school room. If I had been there, I could have shown them where to find the toys in the big cupboards." That reminded me, I still hadn't been upstairs in my heavenly bedroom to see what kinds of toys Steve had to play with.

Uncle Alex pointed to the door at the left of the first landing on the long staircase. The door already had my name on it, right under Steve's name. Steve and Scotty, S and S. We were the "S and S boys" in GG's house! When the door swung open I couldn't believe my eyes. Steve had shelves almost to the ceiling filled with toys and books. He even had a record player. He was sitting on his bed in a Batman costume playing with toy trucks he was driving up and down the bumps and humps he'd made in the quilt. He had a fire truck and a dump truck plus three pick-ups. "Hey," I said to get his attention, "what's that music you're playing?" It sounded familiar.

"Hi, Scotty," he yelled in order to be heard over the music. "That's one of my favorite scary stories, 'Peter and the Wolf.' Wait just a minute and the music will stop so we can hear the story. Your bed's over by the big window. You can put your toys on the empty shelves next to the closet door." My bed in Heaven was covered with a blanket the same as was on my bed in Salem – astronauts walking in their space suits on the moon, or so I guessed because the surface design had holes in it like Swiss cheese. It also showed the lunar rover, American flags with stars, and planets all over the background.

A voice from the record player started telling the wolf story. Steve listened with full attention, but I was more interested in two rows of dinosaurs on his upper shelves. I whispered, "Can I check out your dinosaurs?" and he nodded his okay. I had a few dinosaur books and models back in Salem, but Steve had lots more. "Cool," I said as I named all the ones I could remember: "Stegosaurus with the pointy back, Diplodocus with the longest neck and tail, Brontosaurus who only ate plants and trees, Triceratops with the big horns on his head, and Tyrannosaurus Rex who had mean, bloody teeth and little bitty arms."

The first year we lived in Oregon we went on a family vacation and stopped at a prehistoric animal park on the coast. The life-sized models were huge and scary. You could walk under them or crawl up their necks if you wanted to. When we climbed up on the railing beside the trail, I could put my whole arm in Bronty's mouth. I wasn't afraid because Phillip read the sign that said this one only ate leaves, not people or animals. On another vacation, when I was four, we went to a museum in Victoria, Canada. They had skeletons of some prehistoric monsters, including a killer whale and sharks. When I went back to Little Beavers I took the book Mom bought me and showed all the kids in my group. Rhonda, my teacher, told me how smart I was to remember all the dinosaur names.

While Steve listened to his record story and I remembered our dinosaur trips, the music reminded me how our family sang the radio songs when we drove on our vacations. "You can't roller skate in a buffalo herd…" "Bye, bye Miss American Pie…" "Wake up Little Susie, wake up…" "Like a Bridge Over Troubled Waters…" Daddy really liked Roger Miller and Don McLean. Mom could harmonize with the Everly Brothers and Simon and Garfunkel. I remembered that the words of the "bridge" song were about helping someone who is hurt and unhappy. I wished I could sing it with my family now and help them stop hurting.

Steve lifted the needle off his record and the room was quiet. He swung around in his Bat Man cape and plopped down on the big braid rug between our beds. "So, how come you're in Heaven when you're only four years old?" he inquired. "I got really sick with leukemia when I was three, but I lived on Earth with my family until I was four years, four months and three days old. My family lived on an island and we loved to go to the beach when the sun came out. Do you like the ocean?"

"Yeah, but my family never lived on an island. Did it have palm trees?" I asked.

"No, no, it was in Washington State. No palm trees there. But we had green forests and big snowy mountains," he replied.

"My house in Oregon is in the woods. I lived in Oregon and in New Mexico for four years, four months and nine days. I was almost the same age as you when I died, Steve. I was killed in a car crash. Uncle Alex and I were just watching to see how my funeral day went. My family is missing me and feeling very lonely, especially my brother, Phillip."

"Oh, I had two little sisters, but no brother. You and I can pretend we're brothers now," said Steve.

"We're the S and S boys at GG's house," I announced. "See," I said, pointing at the door, "both our names begin with big curly S's." I continued, "What's leukemia?"

"I have talked that over with Uncle Alex and GG because all three of us died of cancer, just different kinds. The leukemia kind is in your blood, and it made me very tired all the time. I had a high fever and the doctors wanted me to stay in the hospital. They poked me with needles and did lots of tests and treatments." He winced. "My mom couldn't stand to see me in so much pain, so I got to go home on the island for the last four months of my life. Mommy and Daddy held me and my grandpa was there when I died and became an angel."

"I never got to be a real patient in the hospital, only during make-believe when we played rescue and emergency," I explained. "My big brother Phillip was real sick in the Albuquerque hospital when he was a baby. He also got to go to the Emergency Room twice after the accident that killed me. I guess I was just healthy all the time, except for chicken pox. I liked going to the hospital with my doctor dad on Saturdays, but I never went to the part with kid patients. Hey, I have my own stethoscope, but it's back in Oregon, not here."

Steve pushed his Bat Man mask up on his forehead so I could see his big brown eyes. "I was wondering," I said, "have you seen any angels with wings? I don't suppose you have a bat-mobile? How do you get to the far away places around Heaven?"

"We don't need wings here, silly!" he laughed. "That's just in books and paintings and churches down on Earth. We are moved by our spirits, wherever we want to go. Except," he cautioned, "it's not possible to go back to Earth and life as it was before. But you'll get the hang of it and pretty soon you won't even miss not having cars or trains or stuff like that. I have some toys that remind me of planes and ferry boats and travel on Earth, but we just don't have any use for those things here."

Just then we heard a musical chime coming from downstairs and Steve explained that twelve notes meant it was time for lunch. He carefully put all his trucks back on the shelves and smoothed the lumps out of his bed. Seems one of the chores at GG's house was keeping a clean and tidy room. Suited me fine. I liked all my equipment and toys in a safe place where I could find them when I needed them. I was going to have to ask GG and Unk how to get some of my things from Oregon, but now I smelled chicken soup and was happy to head down to the dining room.

Grace at GG's table was everyone's job. On this day Uncle Alex started it off by saying, "We thank God for Scotty, who has joined our heavenly family." We were all holding hands and I peeked to see Unk gently squeeze Gilberto's hand. Gilberto said he was thankful for ladybugs he'd seen in the garden, then squeezed the next kid's hand. Sasha's head was bowed and her voice was soft, but she said she was thankful for chicken noodle soup and bread and butter. Heather said she was thankful for her Barbie doll. That made some of the other kids giggle. Steve told me later that she said the same thing almost every time, three meals a day. At first she had said she was thankful for her baby brother, but remembering her earth family had made her cry. She decided to stick with Barbie, though I could tell she was very happy in her heavenly family now. When it came my turn I had thought of about ten things, but they only wanted to hear one. I thanked God for my new bedroom and Steve, my new "brother."

9 The Solace Stone

After lunch was the time of rest. I don't know if all the kids felt like they wanted a nap, but GG and Unk needed a break. When the dishes were done and things quieted down, the adults went outside in the fresh air to snooze or pick flowers, or maybe to visit with the neighbors next door. I had noticed from the window near my bed that the big treehouse was built in the neighbor's back yard. I hoped the neighbors allowed us little kids to climb up the rope ladder to play in the tree limbs.

That got me thinking about the treehouse Dad had built in our yard, which was puny compared to the one in Heaven. Still, I was dreaming and missing some of the things on Earth. I dreamed about my St. Bernard puppy, Heidi, and how she licked my face all the time. I remembered the Billy goats our neighbor, Larry, got to help "mow" his yard. Sometimes the biggest goat got loose from his chain. He chased me and, if I didn't run fast enough, he butted me over on the ground. The first time I was afraid of his horns and cried, but then I got used to it and running away was a fun game. Once the goat jumped up on the hood of our car and just stood there looking at us through the windshield. He looked so stupid up there we all laughed our heads off.

These dreams of Heidi and the goat suddenly shifted as I realized I was watching my parents on the day after my funeral. Mom stayed home with Phillip so he could rest for another week, doctor's orders. Dad said he would take care of getting a headstone for my grave. They discussed angels and astronauts, trying to envision me flying free somewhere, happy and healthy. Mom suggested a flat marble stone rather than something upright. She had visited her father's grave many times and noticed how the grass was kept tidy if the mower could go over a stone, but it was overgrown and weedy around the base of tall headstones. "Did you notice the grave next to Scotty's?" she asked my dad. "The stone is flat and neat, practical but pretty. The old woman buried there is named Presley, like Elvis, and I'm thinking 'ole Grandma Presley is close by to guide our Scotty beyond death." Dad nodded but made no comment as he headed back to work.

So, Dad ordered a square of red marble to be carved with the following message:

THOMAS JOSEPH SCOTT MAYHALL
MARCH 13, 1973 – JULY 22, 1977
SCOTTY WANTED TO BE AN ASTRONAUT
NOW HE FLIES WITH ANGELS
WE WILL ALWAYS LOVE HIM

I wished I could tell my parents what Steve had told me about flying without wings and without a spaceship. They would be glad to know I was going to fly all over the place now, even if I couldn't grow up to be an astronaut in the real Space Shuttle program.

Grandmother and Granddaddy flew home to Texas on Wednesday. Sue flew back to her nursing job in Rochester, New York. By then Granddaddy had finished making the memory box for my special things. Mom was making a collage of pictures to decorate the top. The box had a neat lock on it and Mom chose a shade of blue to paint the sides and bottom. It wasn't the same "baby" blue like the color of my casket, which had made people cry at the cemetery. Mom hoped the house would not be such a sad place if my things weren't scattered all over as reminders of me being gone for good. She had given away a few of my stuffed animals and drawings to family members who wanted a "Scotty keepsake," but there was still a lot more stuff than would fit in Granddaddy's box.

After Dad left the house for work on Thursday, and while Phillip napped, Mom took Heidi and walked down the bank into our wooded backyard. There were blackberry bushes and poison oak to watch out for, but there was also the spot and the big rock, hidden from the neighbors' view, which Mom called her "solace stone." In the spring she could sit on this rock surrounded by wildflowers, especially trillium and lamb's ear. I went there with her a few times. On a clear day you could look through the trunks of the oaks and Douglas firs to see miles of planted farmland leading to the foothills of the Oregon Coastal Range, which usually had snow on top. Today she perched on the rock as Heidi leaned in on her dangling legs. She let the tears of loneliness gush from her eyes. She couldn't squelch some muffled wails of grief that tore out of her throat. "Scotty, I miss you so much. Oh, God, if I could die to bring him back I would do it in a minute, right now. Help me to get through this pain, God. It hurts so bad."

She slid down the side of the stone onto the ground and into an embrace with Heidi. Those big, sad, St. Bernard eyes seemed to know my mom was very upset. The dog let her wipe her face and her nose in its fur. Pretty soon they started back up the hill, stopping at the treehouse. Mom found a couple pieces of my equipment that I had made and stored there: a twig I'd shaped into a small pistol with a piece of Dad's sandpaper because Mom didn't allow us to have toy guns from the store, and some big bird feathers I'd tied together with a piece of rope so I could wear it as an Indian headband. She carefully carried these back to the house and set them on the window sill in my bedroom. Curling up on my bed, she let the tears flow until she dozed for a nap, making up for the sleeplessness of the nights since I died six days earlier.

Mom, Phillip and Heidi woke up to the sound of the doorbell ringing. They looked out to see Amy, a friend from church, unloading a trunk full of casserole dishes and desserts. Though Mom knew the fridge was already full, she hugged Amy and her little boy, Sam, and helped them bring the food inside. She joked, "Well, we certainly aren't likely to wither away from hunger anytime soon!" The 4Cs moms' group at the Congregational Church had cooked a variety of full meals that would be quick and easy to serve. Mom wondered if they'd ever be able to eat it all before it went to waste.

She thanked Amy, said good-bye, and started trying to rearrange the contents of the refrigerator and freezer, reminiscing about trips to shop for groceries. That was the last thing she wanted to do now, so having plenty of food on hand was a good idea. At first this custom of bringing food had seemed so old-fashioned. It surprised her so that she almost rejected the offers, even though she knew it was a way for caring friends to show their concern in a practical, helpful way.

Mom reflected on how grocery shopping with Phillip and me had become fun times; we played games as Mom scooted the cart from one aisle to the next. Phillip had been going to grocery stores longer than me and he could read all the labels without much trouble. I could only read the ones I recognized from TV commercials. I saw Tony the Tiger and shouted, "Kellogg's Frosted Flakes!" On the cleaning products aisle I could read "Mr. Clean," and I could find the corn and green beans with the "Green Giant" on the label. Mom said out loud and with a lump in her throat, "Greebies...Gweebies," which was a silly name Dad made up for green beans. I had a problem saying "r's" and used "w's" instead, so that made it even funnier. Mom told me I sounded like Elmer Fudd in the movie cartoons. She decided right then that she'd avoid going to the grocery store for awhile, fearing she'd melt into a puddle of tears in the produce section.

Phillip sampled three kinds of the cookies Amy had left. He curled up with Heidi on the beanbag chair to watch "Electric Company" and the "Mickey Mouse Club" on TV. Mom made phone calls to her friends and teachers at OSU to let them know she planned to return to campus the next week. People told her it was too soon, but she said she needed to get back to business and be ready for final exams the second week in August. The long days just hanging around the house were too lonely. There were a few phone calls still coming in. She tried to send thank-you notes or letters to people who sent cards with money for the playground at Little Beavers. Otherwise, the hours went by slowly and she was too sad.

10   Scotty's Life in Oregon

All my new friends in Heaven wanted to know about where I came from, so I called a big pow-wow on the grass beneath a chestnut tree in GG's front yard. "My mom has lots of picture albums of me when I was a baby, but I don't really remember much before we moved in our big U-Haul truck from Gallup, New Mexico to Oregon in 1975. I was two-and-a-half that summer. Phillip and I sat in the middle of the cab, between Dad doing the driving and Mom reading the maps and keeping us busy."

I told the kids how we sang songs with the radio voices. When we drove through the mountains we sang, "Colorado Rocky Mountain High" with John Denver. When we got stuck on a back road trying to find a campground, we sang "Take Me Home, Country Roads." "Oh yeah," I remembered, "we sang 'King of the Road' like Roger Miller, and 'England swings like a pendulum do, bobbies on a bicycle two by two....'"

The truck was full of all our furniture. Our Volkswagen camper van was hooked on with a hitch, and our dog, Sonya, rode in it.

Sonya was both a Husky and a German Shepherd. Dad made a silly word for her, "Shusky." My dad could be real fun and funny sometimes, like when he called us "Goobies," for "good babies" or said "pooper-doopers" when we had dirty diapers or training pants. That got my new friends laughing, too.

"Sonya was a beautiful dog, looking like Cleopatra in the movies with dark lines around her blue eyes. She had a white chest and ears that perked up when she wagged her tail. Mom called her their "first-born" because they got her before Phillip was born in Albuquerque. We had to give her away after about a year in Salem because she got out of the yard and chased the farmer's sheep. He warned he'd have to shoot her. One of Dad's patients said he'd take Sonya to stay indoors and guard his mechanic's shop. After that we just had cats, until we got our Heidi puppy.

"Our Salem house in the woods was really big, but the downstairs wasn't finished yet. Phillip and I each had our own room on the main floor, but the daylight basement was just a huge open space with a cement floor. The house wasn't expensive because it needed a lot of work, but my dad liked to do carpentry and planned to finish the house himself when we had more money. I liked the downstairs the way it was because Phillip and I could ride our Big Wheels and bounce balls against the concrete walls and floor on rainy days when it was cold and muddy outside.

"All our Seattle family dropped by for little visits at our new house. They were so happy we moved closer and didn't live in New Mexico anymore. Granny came from Seattle bringing Christmas presents in December and birthday presents in the spring. Auntie Mary's family came in August and we loved playing with our cousin, Timmy, who was just a year older than Phillip. Uncle Alex and Auntie Ginny brought three of their kids to visit for a few days on their way to Reno.

"My godparents, Art and Sue, were living in Tacoma where Art was a kids' doctor on the army base. They drove down in the wintertime for a ski vacation with us at Timberline Lodge. We all stayed in a cabin at the base of Mt. Hood. It belonged to Mom's first boyfriend in college, David, the guy who showed up early at my memorial service. His family spent time in the cabin during the summer. But, in the winter it was so cold in the cabin we stayed at the top of the mountain by the fireplace at the Lodge whenever we weren't outside in the snow. We stayed there all evening until it was time to go down to the cabin and get under the covers. At the Lodge there was a gentle St. Bernard with a barrel around her neck and I wanted to ride her. I had really fat, orange plastic skis with blue straps that buckled around my boots. First I skied down the hills holding onto Mom's or Sue's legs, but later I learned to do it all by myself."

I told my heavenly friends how Auntie Alice's family came for both Christmas and spring vacations when the boys were not in school. "I got to know the twins and Darren Kelly best because they were the cousins who visited us the most and we also stayed in a motel near their house whenever we went to Seahawk football games in Seattle. The very first summer in Salem, Mom decided to have her bunion fixed. David, the oldest twin who was thirteen, came to live with us and babysit while Mom recovered from surgery. Mom was very cranky because we didn't keep the house clean enough and because her foot ached. But Phillip and I had fun with David who played ball with us, read us lots of stories, and didn't make us eat everything on our plates."

"Did you ever go to school before you died?" Freddy wanted to know. "I got to go to the preschool at the big real estate office where my mother worked in Pensacola."

"I don't know where Pensacola is," I replied, "but I went to a school named Montessori in Salem, and later to preschool in Corvallis, Little Beavers. At Montessori I learned to do all kinds of things easily, like tying knots and bows, piling blocks so the biggest one was on the bottom and the littlest way up on top, sanding and polishing wood so it was shiny, and hammering nails. Phillip had a hard time doing most of this stuff, but he was only five and the teacher told my parents he could read as well as fifth graders. Then I went to Little Beavers for a whole year before I got killed. I went to Sunday school, too, where we did a lot of coloring and singing."

That afternoon I wanted to meet the neighbor who had the treehouse in Heaven so I only told the kids a little bit about the year I was at Little Beavers. "I started going there when I was three-and-a-half, just before Uncle Alex died. Phillip was already five so he was in the kindergarten part of the program. My mom's best friend at college had a son my size named Adrian who went to Little Beavers, too. Boy, they had all kinds of stuff to play with and things to do. We could practice being in real school, we cooked a lot of treats for snack time, we played pretend paramedics, everyone got to choose a different drum or horn in music circle, and we had an adding machine so I could play store and handle the money. Every week we went to the big gym at Oregon State where we climbed on the ropes and balance beams, and learned how to get over the obstacle course. I was the only one in my group who could hit the ball with a bat. I loved taking things for show-and-tell, like my dinosaur toys and the hummingbird's nest from the tree outside my bedroom. Rhonda, my teacher, told my folks she had to work hard finding new things to challenge me so I wouldn't get bored."

"I can climb the ropes, too," announced Freddy. "There's a rope ladder up to the treehouse in Uncle Bob's back yard. He lets us play there if we get permission from GG and Uncle Alex." That was just what I wanted to hear. I ended the pow-wow and went to find Unk or GG.

11 *Uncle Bob and the Treehouse*

Unk knew what I was going to ask even before I opened my mouth. "Sure," he said, "now's a good time for you to get to know Uncle Bob next door." Steve and Freddy wanted to go along, but the other kids headed for the porch where GG was serving popsicles for afternoon snack time. As we approached the garden gate in front of the humongus yellow house, Unk called out, "Bob, I have somebody you'll want to meet."

This guy with bushy gray hair, eyebrows and moustache came out the front door hand-in-hand with a short, smiling lady. He looked a lot like pictures in some of Mom's books. At first I thought it was Huckleberry's Mark Twain, but he also looked like Albert Schweitzer. Mom had a whole row of books about Schweitzer, her favorite hero. She told Phillip and me about this doctor who worked with African people in the jungle. When she spoke at church during Time for Children she wore a pith helmet like Albert's and handed out bookmarks she'd made with his picture and a quote about loving and serving poor people like Jesus did. I always wanted to meet him and it looked like now was my chance.

"This is Cheron Joy's youngest son, Scotty, who came to live with us a few days ago. He's been admiring the treehouse your heavenly family made in the giant maple tree out back," Unk announced.

"Oh, what a joy to meet Cheron Joy's boy!" he exclaimed with a chuckle and a twinkle in his blue eyes. He introduced the lady as his wife, Helen Wettleson. She had rosy cheeks, a soft voice, and small feet in high-heeled shoes. "You can call me Uncle Bob or RWW or Mr. Wettleson...your choice. Some of the grown-ups here call me RWW by my initials, and your mother always called us Mr. or Mrs. Wettleson because that was the proper way to address teachers in her high school. Most of the young people in Heaven just call me Uncle Bob, even though none of them was related to me on Earth."

"Okay Uncle Bob," I said. "So, you're telling me you're not Albert Schweitzer? I thought Albert would have made it to Heaven for sure. Where'd he go?"

"Not to worry, Scotty. Albert and his wife, Helene, live over near the Worship Center. He's not a missionary doctor here because angels don't get sick or injured. Instead he's an organist. He practices on the big pipe organ at the Center next to his house.

Everyone's invited to his weekly concerts. Helen and Helene are very good friends, as are Albert and I," explained Uncle Bob. "I'm so pleased your mom told you about Albert while you were on Earth. She and I both believe that he made the world a far better place while he was alive. He spent his lifetime doing good works, mostly for very poor people in Africa. If you're interested, I could introduce you to the Schweitzers when they come to our house for lunch. That doesn't happen very often because Helen and I share our home with eight teenage angels but the Schweitzers aren't that crazy about young people. They are very serious and our house is often in a bit of an uproar."

"How come you have so many teenagers? I have a bunch of teenage cousins back on Earth and I don't think my grandmother and granddaddy could stand sharing space with them for very long at a time."

Uncle Bob smiled broadly and nodded toward GG who was surrounded by popsicle-licking kids on her porch next door. "It may be GG's influence that got us to taking in teens. Helen and I met GG one day when she was getting groceries for a week. It was a lot of food, and we asked why she needed so much. That's when we learned how GG opened her big house to young children who got to Heaven way ahead of their parents and grandparents, uncles and aunts. She invited us to dinner at her place, and we were enchanted by the curious and imaginative little ones around the supper table. We weren't sure we had the energy to keep up with preschoolers, but we thought teen-angels might be fun to share our home with.

"It wasn't until we moved to this big house next door to GG that I discovered the connection between us. While pruning the roses in our back yards, GG told me she'd lived a few years on Beacon Hill in Seattle and her grandchildren went to Franklin High School where Helen and I were on the faculty. And, last year, when Alex arrived here, I realized that I'd seen him somewhere, and his height was a tip-off. He played center for the basketball team and sang in the Franklin choir, usually towering above the heads of the rest of the bass section."

"That seemed quite a coincidence," Unk chimed in. "On Earth we would have exclaimed, 'It's a small world!' In Heaven we just call it 'destiny or God's plan' – that Cheron's favorite teacher and her beloved grandma and brother ended up being next-door neighbors."

Uncle Bob continued, "We arranged this three-level house so Helen and I could live on the main floor, four boys could live downstairs, and four girls each have a room with a good view on the third floor. One of our first projects as a heavenly family was to build the big treehouse. That was in no small measure due to our hope that GG's children would come over to play. It works out well because our yard and our maple tree are perfect for that purpose, while GG has a big vegetable garden and some geese out back. The kids have to be careful when they play not to trample the carrots, green beans and strawberries. As soon as Alex moved in over there he put up a backboard and hoop so the teens could play basketball. He's a good teacher and most of them have already learned to make free throws and jump shots."

I could see that Steve and Freddy adored Uncle Bob and Helen because they had gone right ahead and taken one of their hands. I expected I would be friends with them too, even if they weren't Dr. and Mrs. Albert Schweitzer.

"Are any of the big kids here? I don't hear any music or noise coming from your house. No ruckus going on right now," I observed.

"All ten of us gather for morning and evening meals and we expect all the teens to sleep in their rooms to renew their spirits every night. Otherwise, they are free to explore the universe and do whatever teen-angels like to do. To make OUR heaven perfect, Helen and I needed thousands of books to read, and that's exactly what we got. We believe one of the greatest joys and gifts is to share good books with others. Our teens have discovered that reading, writing and discussing stories is more fun than sitting idle and accomplishing nothing. You'll see," he said, motioning above his head, "we have books on shelves stacked from floor to ceiling in nearly every room of our house. The main floor looks as much like a library as a home."

"Hey, Uncle Bob, do you know I can read now?" I said with pride. " I want to read all your books if that's okay with you and Mrs. Wettleson. Right now I'm wondering if it's all right for Steve, Freddy and me to play in the treehouse. We'll be careful and we promise not to disturb anyone. Please?"

"That's what it's there for, boys. If it's okay with GG and Alex, it's fine with us. Let's have Alex go with you this first time so he can answer any questions you have. Do you have time right now, Alex?" he asked.

"Nothing I'd rather do," Unk replied. "I never got to play with Scotty and Phillip in their treehouse in Salem. It was so small I would have had to stay hunched and my long legs would have taken up all the floor space. The teens here in Heaven built our maple treehouse so they could stand up and so all the little ones could be inside at the same time. It's very roomy!"

The four of us hurried to the huge maple in the far corner of Uncle Bob's enormous back yard. Freddy and Steve with their bare feet scrambled up the rope ladder with ease. Unk gave me a boost so I started my climb halfway up and was on top in a jiffy. The treehouse was made of wood with knots in it, which Unk told me was "knotty pine." "In the house where I grew up in Seattle, the walls and ceilings of the upstairs bedrooms were the same kind of wood," Unk noted. "Being in this treehouse reminds me of my childhood home. Our neighborhood kids on Beacon Hill also built a little treehouse in the woods below our street. We put a roof on it so we could stay dry from Seattle rains but it was always leaking and the floor had puddles of water except during the summer.

"Once Scotty's mom, Cheron, told me a funny secret about playing in that treehouse," said Uncle Alex, addressing all three of us little boys. "I kept her secret all these years, but now I think it's a good story to share and she wouldn't mind. Seems she and a couple of her little girlfriends, about eight years old, wanted to try smoking like the glamorous movie actresses. Cigarettes were absolutely forbidden in our house so they decided to make their own out of tree twigs. They peeled twigs that were about the size of cigarettes and hid them under a floorboard to dry. Later one of the girls brought a book of matches and the three of them lit up. Cheron told me they reclined in poses like Gloria Swanson and Katharine Hepburn to look sophisticated as they smoked, but they had to puff real hard to keep the twigs burning and they couldn't stop coughing because it scorched their throats. Cheron decided right then that twig smoking wasn't worth the trouble. To save face and not look like a sissy, she lectured the other two about the hazards of lighting matches in the woods during the hot summer. Our mom would have spanked Cheron if she'd found out about the smoking and matches, but she never did."

"Smoking is BAD!" I shouted. "Everybody knows it can kill you. We wouldn't try a trick like that, would we boys?" Steve and Freddy wagged their heads back and forth in agreement. "I'd rather bring a snack up here. Then we could all sit around in a circle with crossed legs like Indians, telling stories or having show-and-tell with our toys and books. No peace-pipe smoking though! Hey, I'm wondering about Uncle Bob and his wife. Mom never told me about them. Do they come up here in the treehouse sometimes?"

We all made ourselves comfortable on some cushions we dragged to a shady spot on the big knotty pine platform. The leaves of the maple were as big as frisbees so there was plenty of shelter from the hot sun. Uncle Alex called down to Uncle Bob and he climbed the rope ladder to join our pow-wow. I loved pow-wows and could hardly wait to see what stories this new guy had to tell. I noticed he was now wearing cowboy boots with his jeans and plaid shirt. "Where'd you get those shiny boots?" I asked.

"Ha!" he laughed, slapping his leg with delight. "When I saw you in your boots I remembered how much I used to enjoy wearing mine. They've been lost in my closet because most angels go barefoot and I can't remember the last time I saw feet in boots. Anyhow, I used to work at Longacres race track on weekends and summers to supplement my teacher's pay. Instead of a suit or sports coat, which I always wore to teach at Franklin, I could relax in comfortable clothes." Now I thought he looked more like Pa Cartwright on "Bonanza." All he needed was a cowboy hat and a horse.

A large, gray cat came slinking along a branch of the tree, jumped into our circle, and nuzzled up against Uncle Bob's leg. "This critter we call 'Houdini' because he does tricks. In fact, he is just like the cat we had on Earth. His most amazing trick is opening the front door. He learned to jump up and grab the door knob with his front paws so that it turned and the door opened. I remember the first time Cheron saw Houdini let himself in. We'd invited my editors from the student newspaper to come to the house on a Sunday afternoon so we could brainstorm fresh ideas for the spring issues. As we all sat around the fireplace Houdini started his doorknob routine. Cheron noticed his antics out the window from where she was sitting. She pointed and laughed out loud, just about the time the cat succeeded and strutted smartly through the hallway and into the living room. So, here in Heaven we have a similar door and knob so this kitty can continue to keep us all laughing."

"Oh yeah," I remembered, "Mom told me about that smart cat, but I don't remember anything else she told me about you and your wife. So, you dressed up like a cowboy to work at the horse races, and you dressed like a businessman to teach at the high school. What else did you do back when you were on Earth with my mom?"

"Mostly I taught high school journalism, and I advised the students who published the weekly newspaper, the Franklin TOLO. Cheron was a good writer and a serious student. She became a better writer and more self-confident when she started reading good books and learned to think for herself and express her opinions. I was famous for trying any tactic to get students to be thoughtful and creative, rather than passive learners.

"Back in the 50's and 60's I got very frustrated with high schoolers sitting in classes like frogs or knots on a log. The 'live' ones – frogs – might at least flick their tongues from time to time if something I said caught their attention. Now and then they responded intelligently. Too many students were more like the knots – unresponsive. Most teachers were satisfied with 'information in – information out' learning. It's called 'rote' learning. I wanted my students to be creative and courageous, not compliant.

"I felt compelled to provoke them. I was known to yell or throw erasers at students who dozed off. I really succeeded in getting their attention one day when I started tossing my own books out of the third floor window of the school. I named each book by title and author, said 'Going, going, gone', then tossed the book if no one spoke up to borrow it. I had been begging them for weeks to take home some of my books by great thinkers and writers like Carl Sandburg, Thomas Jefferson, C.S. Lewis, John Milton, Mark Twain, Hemingway and Faulkner. To my dismay, the shelves and chalk trays around the room remained filled with my books…no takers. Boy, after that tossing-out-the-window incident, every single student left class with a book or two."

"My teachers at Montessori and Little Beavers told us never to throw books. Did you get into trouble that day?" I asked.

"Sure, Scotty, I was in trouble with the principal much of the time," Uncle Bob confessed with a devilish grin. "But some of the students, like your mother, began reading and thinking and writing about the most important things they'd have to face in the adult world, like freedom and war, caring about racial discrimination and needy people, hypocrisy and lack of moral conviction." He paused and shook his wise old head. "Sorry…I'm on my bandwagon. I'm lecturing you with stuff much too serious for a sunny day in the treehouse with three precious little boys. Let's go down and get some of GG's popsicles and have some fun before suppertime."

Unk, Freddy and Steve all slid down a rope like a fireman's pole for a fast getaway while Uncle Bob and I climbed down the rope ladder in our boots. I hugged his legs and thanked him for letting us play in his yard and for loving my mom and telling me about her as a kid.

12 Returning to Corvallis; Confronting Death's Realities

By early August, Mom and Phillip were feeling stronger and they were tired of being around the house all day, everyday. Even though I had been dead only ten days, most other people were back at work or school, or whatever, acting like nothing had ever happened. Except at church on Sundays. Everyone noticed that I was not there in my Sunday school group. And I wasn't up front by the altar asking questions when the minister led the Time for Children. Mom decided to sit way in the back because she cried during the praying and singing. Sylvia, one of Mom's friends, sat in church with her when Daddy was working because she knew Mom was going to need Kleenex and a shoulder to cry on.

On Monday morning Mom and Phillip drove south to Corvallis where he was dropped off at Little Beavers. Mom told him, "I can't take you inside this morning because I know I'll bawl when I see Scotty's teacher or the kids in his group." She hugged Phillip tight and told him to give an envelope full of playground money to Jan East. Then Mom turned the car quickly and headed toward the university, refusing to cry on the first day back to classes. It turned out to be a good day. All her friends and teachers on campus were either counselors or studying to be counselors. They'd thought a lot about how they'd welcome Mom back and make her comfortable. They had already formed some study groups to help her catch up and get ready for final exams the next week. They let her talk about me and the accident if she wanted to, but mostly they stuck to the school business.

The second day back on campus wasn't bad either. Mom thought she was strong enough to go by the hospital in the afternoon to visit Carla, the lady who was driving when the car crashed and I was killed. Mom didn't want to blame Carla or see her suffering and guilty. She sat in the hospital parking lot and rehearsed what she might say: "We know it was an accident...How are your twins doing?...We hope you are discharged soon...". She took a deep breath and walked up to the information desk to ask, "What room is Carla Norris in?" When the helper lady said, "Oh, she was sent home yesterday," Mom just about collapsed with a sense of relief. She wasn't ready to face Carla yet. She ran out to the car, holding back the flood of tears, and drove straight to Little Beavers.

Jan East and Rhonda saw Mom pull in and press her forehead against her arms crossed over the steering wheel. She was crying so hard they had to go out and rescue her. Inside Little Beavers it was cooler on that hot summer day. Mom could relax a bit and get her control back. She didn't want to upset the kids, but most of them had already gone home for the day. Phillip came to comfort her, and Rhonda had a folder of my artwork and writing, and some things I made in crafts class: a poster with my handprints in many colors; a bottle with pink tissue paper glued on it for a bud vase; a tie-dye cloth I had made for a placemat. That really started everyone bawling, so they brought some iced tea and all sat for awhile until Mom quieted down.

Phillip kept his hand on Mom's arm during the trip home. She smiled her thanks to him. He hated to see her cry so much. When they passed the Suver intersection where the accident had happened ten days earlier, Mom explained to Phillip what she knew about the wreck so he could understand better what had happened to him that night. She wanted to stop by and talk with the people in the gas station and general store. They would know more details. She wanted to know the truth about how I died. But, for today, she had put herself through enough misery and knew they'd best get home to start dinner for Dad.

Some of our friends had asked Dad if he wanted to take legal action against Carla, but that didn't make sense to my parents. My Dad said, "It's a bad situation you can't turn into something positive. As we say in Texas, 'You can't make chicken salad out of chicken shit!'" Mom said, "Guess we're supposed to take the 'lemons' in our lives and try to make lemonade." But, no amount of money or effort could make me alive again, and Carla didn't have any money anyway. Instead, Mom and Dad talked about the danger of that highway intersection and decided to ask the highway department to make it safer. They sent some letters and were waiting for answers.

On August 8, our Pastor Ed returned from his trip to the Holy Lands and came right out to see our family. Mom apologized because she felt like a zombie that day. She had been reading some of the books in her library that she thought would give her strength. Someone had given her a little book written by a minister who seemed to think God had planned for me to die. "He suggests that Scotty would have grown into a bad person so this was a way of saving us pain later," Mom explained. "Can you imagine God acting like that?"

Ed was a very wise man and quick to deny that God would arrange my death. "Cheron, this was one of those horrible accidents that happen here on Earth, with no rhyme or reason. Scotty is precious in God's eyes. God does not want your family to suffer such loss and sadness. He is not cruel and unmerciful." Then he prayed for comfort and understanding, He sat with my family in silence for a long time. He hugged Phillip and allowed Heidi to lick his hand. He let my parents know he was available if they needed him. There was nothing more he could say or do.

After the pastor left Mom decided to write down some of her thoughts:

        Our Scotty – "Angel-Astronaut"

He was such a beautiful and perfect little person in every way: happy, loving, inquisitive, creative, intelligent, fearless, capable, healthy. He had the potential to achieve anything he desired in life, and his enthusiasm for a wide variety of activities was abundant.

Most recently he had set his sights on being an astronaut – a "space commander." He was really hooked on "Space 1999" and so delightfully excited by "Star Wars"- R2D2, Chewbacca and C3P0. He eagerly looked forward to the August 12th launch of the "real" Space Shuttle program.

There were times when he would have settled for being a paramedic or cowboy or a sea diver with Jacques Cousteau, but at age 4, he was "star struck" and his fascination with the prospects of space exploration was endless.

But August never came for Scotty, at least not within the span of his earthly life. It ended in the fourth year, fourth month, ninth day: July 22, 1977. What an immeasueable, unexplainable loss!

Scotty was a most lovely gift, given to us for only a few short years. Everyone who knew him was blessed by the love and joy which he so freely shared. It would truly be a fitting tribute if we could all get in touch with the purity and innocence of that love he gave to us, and then share it generously with all other living creatures we might meet.

No, Scotty never lived to be an astronaut. But we

like to think of him – crooked wings, tarnished halo, belted robes and cowboy boots – flying with the angels, sailing and soaring across the Heavens with complete abandon, free as a bird and filled with unbounded joy and happiness. ----- Cheron, August 8, 1977

I looked back and noticed Uncle Alex and Uncle Bob looking over my shoulder as I read what Mom was writing. "That's beautiful," said Uncle Bob. "She is trying to settle her heart and memory to make sense out of your loss and not be destroyed by the belief that it's all over for you. Aren't you glad that she has an inkling of how you're getting on in Heaven?"

I pondered aloud, "She knows about little boy angels because of reading *The Littlest Angel* so many times every Christmas. Did you know that the kid in the book lived 'exactly four years, six months, five days, seven hours and forty-two minutes'...almost the same as Steve and me? I memorized that part. And, he had a box full of his special earthly things, like his dog's collar and some shiney stones from the stream bank by his house. I'll bet that's where Mom got the idea of having Granddaddy make a box to store my special stuff."

"Oh," said Uncle Bob, "your mom seemed drawn to reading many books and plays that were about death and loss. It was not an uncommon theme in the books I tried to get students to read. So many of the teenagers I taught believed they were invincible and hadn't ever experienced death in their families. Your mom had lost her dad when she was very young, GG was sick with cancer much of the time when she was a teen, and she told me about the little boy she babysat who had spina bifida and died at age four. She also cared for malnourished children as a Peace Corps Volunteer and in an Oregon migrant labor camp. A few of them had died. Your mom had to develop a concept of death that would not devastate her. I think it is helping her now to get used to losing you.

"In my class alone she read and wrote reports on the writings of other parents who had lost children: John and Frances Gunther – *Death be Not Proud*; William Allen White's famous editorial after his daughter, Mary, died when a tree branch knocked her off her horse; the role of a mother she'd enacted for a speech and drama contest which won her the gold medal, *All My Sons* by Arthur Miller, in which a family mourns the death of their soldier son; *A Death in the Family* by James Agee, wherein a mom tries to explain to her children about their father's death. Cheron had a knack for personalizing what she read and making it relevant to her own life."

Uncle Alex said, "I've been watching your mom these past few days as she contemplates the possibility of angels and life after death. I'm sure believing in angels seems less important when those who die have had a full life, but it's harder to think that there's nothing more after a little child dies. I remember when GG died, your mom was only nineteen and away at college, but she wrote a very thoughtful poem and came home to Seattle to read it at the memorial service. She wrote:

Upon Grandma's Death, 7/14/63

Who can judge when life is full and complete,
And, when death comes, if it is bitter or sweet?
Each man alone must check and test his fate
And judge if death comes soon, or much too late.

I think a just criterion might be
To ponder on the thought of Love to see
How much had been expelled each living day...
How much of us we leave along the way.

She seemed to be figuring out back then that the measure of a good life was sharing love each and every day. If we do that it's not so bad to die young."

"I love my Mommy very much," I said, with a little choke in my throat. "I loved her every day. And I miss her every day, even though I like Heaven so far. It's good that her thinking of me as an angel makes her happy, but I hope she isn't so happy that she will forget me altogether."

"No chance of that," Unk assured me. "You are a part of her heart forever. Same goes for your dad, Phillip and lots of other people you shared your love and earthly life with."

Right at that instant all three of us – Unk, Uncle Bob and I – realized that Mom was in a dream state down there on Earth. She was envisioning me as an angel in the care of her grandma, her brother and her best teacher ever, Mr Wettleson, alias Uncle Bob. We three guys all hugged and were happy to see this awakening, even while dreaming! Unk elbowed my side and said, "If she only knew, eh Scotty!? Remember I told you on that first day we met in Heaven, how we'd all help you adjust and help your left-behind family to go on with their lives as well. You, Scotty, just established the 'love link' between Heaven and Earth, and that helps your mom and others to understand the connection with more clarity and peace.

"We're going to have a good life here in Heaven; your family is going to be able to get past this tragedy and go on to make a good life on Earth. We'll all be ready and waiting for them when their days on Earth come to an end. Won't that be a grand reunion for all of us?"

13   Yellow Mercedes

Mom's student friend, Satsuki, was amazed at how Mom was able to study and learn the material for her final exams. Mom explained that she had learned to "compartmentalize" and focus so her brain could work well even if her emotions were in turmoil. She was able to pass all of her tests but took an incomplete in one course so she could finish the term paper that was required. Finals week was not easy, but Mom was glad she'd not have to face a bunch of unfinished work between August and the start of fall quarter. Now that I was dead and not going to Little Beavers anymore, and Phillip was going to start first grade in Salem, Mom was hoping to make the drive to Corvallis only two or three days a week. She had finished her assistantship teaching Masters-level counseling students. She only needed one more class during fall term, plus lots of work on her dissertation research project. She would also have to prepare for comprehensive written and oral exams in the spring.

Dad encouraged Mom to take a weekend break with Phillip and go to the Oregon coast, even though he had to stay and work at the hospital. Satsuki made time to go along. One of the professors gave them the keys to her vacation house on Little Whale Cove. Dad gave Mom the keys to his Mitsubishi sports car so they'd have some fun and be comfortable on the drive. It was white with fancy blue and red stripes. Dad figured the light color could be seen better by other drivers and was safer. Dad loved Mom a lot to let her drive his racy car! He was now back to being very busy with his doctor work. He worried that Mom didn't have enough to keep her busy and get beyond her sadness now that the college term was ended.

I watched them at the coast and Mom had some problems, that's for sure. When they went into the town to shop, Mom crashed the front bumper of the Mitsubishi on a high curb. At first she wanted to cry, but Satsuki got her laughing about how unimportant it was in the big picture of all that was happening. They walked in the sunshine and fresh air of the sandy beaches where Phillip gathered a bag of seashells and stones. Hanging around the beach house, talking, it was going pretty well until Mom went to the bathroom and suddenly started shaking and crying real hard. Phillip ran to her as she sat on the side of the bathtub. His hugs and "I love yous" seemed to make her feel a lot better.

Dad was back in Salem that weekend spending his spare time shopping for a safer car. He decided Mom and Phillip should be as free from danger as possible when they were driving around. My parents always shopped carefully for a good deal before they paid a lot of money but Dad didn't seem to care about anything but safety this time. He found a new yellow Mercedes with a diesel engine, top-ranked for safety. He decided to buy it and surprise Mom when she came back from the beach.

I ran to tell Unk that Mom was going to get a fancy yellow car. "Wow, a Mercedes!" he exclaimed and whistled. I whistled too. "Your mom is going to worry about the price, but she will know that he loves her too much not to pay any price at all to see that his family is as safe as can be on the road."

"Okay," I said to Uncle Alex. "Steve and I are going to have a pow-wow now to talk about my gear and toys. Can I get copies of all the stuff I had to leave behind? Steve is very good at sharing but I have some things on Earth I'm sure we could have fun with. I need my belts and ropes and walkie-talkies. Oh, and my penny collection and wallet, and my helicopter toy and Honey Bear…"

"GG and I will work at getting the things you desire to have happiness and fun here in Heaven. You and Steve make a list and we'll see what we can do," Uncle Alex assured me. So I headed upstairs while GG and Unk took over the watchman's job to be sure my Earth family was okay.

"I think their grief work is coming along pretty well, don't you?" GG asked Unk. "They're functioning to get on with life while still letting the memories warm them and the tears relieve their pain. Losing one of only two children leaves a huge hole in the family unit."

"They've been regretting Bill's vasectomy and wishing they could try to have another baby," Unk said. "All Cheron's sociology training, and her experiences with overpopulation and poverty in Latin America and on the Navajo reservation, caused her to join the Zero Population Growth group and pledge to have only two children. But they never wanted to raise an only child, never.

"Now she's been reading some books about parental bereavement and how to get beyond the loss of a child. Some of the studies say that many parents who lose a young child don't want to have sex because it reminds them of conceiving the child they lost, or something like that. Some couples can't get beyond blaming one another, and that drives them apart."

"Fortunately," smiled GG, "that doesn't seem to be a hang-up for Bill and Cheron. Their sex life continues to be healthy. I'm so glad of it. They need to grow closer together through this crisis rather than drifting apart."

Unk and GG saw how Mom loved Dad for buying her a safer car, and she got a kick out of the yellow color he'd chosen. Dad was color-blind and had big problems with greens and reds, so blues and yellows were safer for him to choose, as well as safer for the driver and passengers. They took a little spin around Salem in the new car after the bashed up Mitsubishi got home from the beach. Mom apologized, but Dad just said he'd get it fixed and wasn't mad at all. GG observed how, after they'd tucked Phillip into his bed, they hugged and kissed a lot and found comfort in their closeness.

14 Memories and Keepsakes

It was almost a month after I died when Dr. Chester called my mom into his office and started telling her how much he missed having me stop by. He and I had some really good talks about the bone-doctor business, but he always wanted to know what I thought about Star Wars and dinosaurs and what I was learning at my school, too. He gave me a stethoscope and he was teaching me to tell time on my Mickey Mouse watch.

"Cheron," he began, "you must know how remarkable Scotty was in every respect. Why, I never ever saw a child who was so completely balanced. His little body worked so well for him. He was always eager to show me how he'd learned to skip, or whistle or wink. Sometimes he'd sing me a new song they'd taught him at school, from start to finish. He was proud to know all the words, even though he couldn't read yet. Recently he showed me how he'd learned to tie his shoes. He said he was teaching the other kids in his class.

"I've raised a few of my own children and had many little ones as patients in my medical practice, but none ever held a candle to Scotty's intelligence and confidence in his own abilities. Only God knows why his short life has ended. People have said, 'God only takes the best and brightest,' and I guess it's the truth in this instance. I'm so sorry we've lost him."

Mom was really bawling with these memories, but she told Dr. Chester it felt good to know that other people loved and missed me still. There weren't very many comforting phone calls or letters coming in now that the shock and the funeral were all over with.

After this talk with Dr. Chester – John – Mom went home to work on the memory box Granddaddy had built for my stuff. Phillip was spending the afternoon with a family from our church who had kids, so she was alone with time to start sorting through my belongings to see what would fit in the box. She smiled or cried as she handled each thing. She arranged them on top of my bed:

> Honey Bear, my teddy from Grandmother and
>   Granddaddy in Texas
> "Emergency" hat and MASH helicopter with a red cross on it
> Parachute Man and Frog Man
> Six Matchbox cars and Mickey Mouse ears and watch
> My leather wallet from the dude ranch, and my bunny
>   bank and penny collection
> Two belts with gear attached – ropes, sunglasses, keys,
>   homemade gun and a clothespin
> Stethoscope and walkie-talkie
> Clothes like my necktie, the red vest Grandmother knitted,

    Kermit the Frog slippers
    My baby toy, a wind-up giraffe that played a lullabye
    Black yarn wig Mom made for my Frankenstein Halloween
        costume, and neck bolts with suction cups on them
    My favorite puzzles and books I wrote my whole name on
    Crafts I made in school: a necklace with a clay turtle
        hanging on it, a bud vase with pink tissue paper for
        Mothers Day, a tie-dye cloth and a placemat with my
        hand prints
    The plastic AVON bottles in the shapes of T-Rex,
        Diplodocus and Brontosaurus

    It was a lot of stuff, but Mom made it all fit inside the blue box with the special lock on the outside. On top of the box she had decoupaged a bunch of pictures of me from the time I was a baby until the last month of my life, and a copy of my name that I wrote all by myself. By the time she finished deciding what to keep forever in the memory box, Mom seemed to feel better and she wasn't crying anymore.

    I decided to tell GG and Uncle Alex that I'd be happy if they would help me get most of the same toys and equipment my mom had chosen for the box. Also, I wanted to have my blankie that went underground with my body in the coffin. I wouldn't need the clothes or the gifts I made for Mommy and Daddy. GG thought I'd made good choices and I found every last thing waiting for me in my room the next time I went upstairs. Steve helped me arrange it all on my shelves. He told me I could have his dinosaur models to put beside mine, but he wanted my Matchbox cars to put on his shelves with his toy trucks. Seemed like a good trade to me. Besides, we made a pact to let each other play with any of the toys whenever we wanted, without getting permission. If the other kids in our heavenly family wanted to use our stuff they'd need to ask nicely, but we were the S and S boys, like brothers, and we thought we'd share everything, fair and square.

We'd planned our big Mayhall family vacation for the summer of 1977: a late-August trip to New Mexico, Texas and Oklahoma City. We had lots of friends there, mostly from medical school in Texas or from Dad's years of orthopedic training in Albuquerque, Truth or Consequences and Gallup. Of course, my grandparents were living in Austin and Dad had an older brother in college at the University of Texas. Mom had bought plane tickets for four; now they could use only three of them. They considered cancelling the whole trip and staying home, but everyone down south wanted to see them and they knew they'd be happier there than at home in Oregon.

They drove around in a rented car and stayed with friends in about six different cities. Almost all the families had kids around the ages of Phillip and me, which made Mom feel sad and miss me more. But she was comforted by having old friends around, fussing over the family and remembering me with funny stories. They remembered I was a very active baby, trying to swim in the middle of the living room floor where there wasn't any water. I could swim in the pool with floaties on my arms. I crawled all over the house when I was seven months old, and started walking at eight-and-a-half months. We were living then in Truth or Consequences, the desert area of New Mexico. Mom said she was glad I was up and walking rather than lying or crawling on the floor where scorpions and centipedes sometimes appeared.

While they were staying with the grandparents in Austin, Dad and Granddaddy talked about the memorial playground. The plan was to develop it in three sections: Past, Present and Future. The Past would look like the Old West pioneer days, with a fort, a covered wagon and an Indian teepee. The Present would include a new paved path all around the buildings for riding bikes and trikes; there would be slides and swings, a carpentry corral and a pet area for the rabbits and guinea pigs. For the Future, Granddaddy was planning to design a space capsule called the "USS Scotty

Mayhall," which would bounce on springs and have instrument panels and walkie-talkies inside so the kid-astronauts could pretend-talk with Mission Control. It was going to be very cool and my Little Beavers friends would have more fun than ever. I was going to have to figure out how to make the "love link" work so I could play with them in spirit.

By the time they ended their vacation visits Mom had lots more money for the playground. They talked about it on the plane ride home. Phillip told them he hoped there would be money to buy some new books for the Little Beavers library because he'd read all of the books. That was his favorite thing to do in free time, after finishing with his kindergarten group. Phillip was proud about his reading and he liked to show off by reading to the little kids, which the teachers loved and appreciated.

15 *The First Day of School*

Phillip was ready for first grade when school opened in September. He was signed up at Eola School, which was an old, two-room building just two miles from our house. All the first graders were in the same class with the second and third graders. Fourth and fifth graders were together in a room right next door. Phillip had met his teacher, Mrs. Down, on registration day in June. He'd told me she was pretty, happy and nice.

The Tuesday after Labor Day Phillip woke up early and got into his school clothes all by himself. He saw lots of fog outside his bedroom window so he was glad his souvenir shirt from the dinosaur park had long sleeves. Dad had kissed Phillip and wished him a good first day of school before he left early for the operating room. Compared to Phillip's excited jabbering, Mom seemed quiet and sad as she made cocoa and sliced bananas into bowls of Cheerios and milk.

"Did you remember to put a tangerine without seeds in my lunchbox, Mom?" asked Phillip. "I don't want any celery today, okay? Did you put apricot jam in my peanut butter sandwich? These new shoes hurt my toe a little bit. Heidi's going to be real lonely today with Scotty gone and me gone." He reached down from his stool at the breakfast bar and scratched the huge puppy's ears. "I'm going to ride the school bus, Heidi, but it will bring me back home at three o'clock and I will play with you then. Mom, do you think they have seatbelts on the bus?"

Mom felt a sudden rush of fear, swallowed hard, then tried to give a reassuring answer. "The governor has been trying to get a seat belt law for school buses in Oregon, but it hasn't happened yet. But you mustn't worry, Phillip. Just stay in your seat and do everything the driver tells you to do. You'll only be going a few miles to pick up other children who will become your new friends. Most kids like riding the yellow buses. I always walked to school when I was a child, so this will be an experience you'll have to tell me all about. I'll walk down the hill to meet you at two-thirty. I think the sunshine should be out before then."

Mom helped Phillip get into his new hooded jacket. He had a hard time with zipping and tying. It was a good thing his new shoes had Velcro instead of tie-up laces. Mom told him he looked like "three million bucks" as they walked down the driveway hand-in-hand. Heidi whimpered as she watched them through the dining room window. Early fallen leaves crunched underfoot until they reached the paved roadway. When the crunching stopped they heard voices and looked through the curtain of fog to see three walkers approaching.

In the seven weeks since the accident, Mom hadn't spent much time thinking about Carla and her twins. Now the three emerged from the dense fog, seemingly ghostlike and haunting. Mom felt a sharp pain in her stomach and struggled to catch her breath. The boy was using crutches and Carla's arm was in a sling. There had been no preparation for this encounter and the strained silence was eerie. The two women made eye contact, then Mom looked quickly at the children and finally managed to say, "Good morning all you first graders. Are you excited about starting school at Eola?"

"We're going to ride the school bus," said Phillip, "but you better hang on and stay in your seat because they don't have seatbelts yet."

The three little ones picked up their pace seemingly unhampered by one on crutches. Carla said something about being sorry for the accident. Mom told her she was glad all three of them were healing and the twins were in shape to start school on time.

Otherwise they just listened to the children's happy conversation in anticipation of the bus ride and the day they were going to spend with Mrs. Down. When the bus came right on time, Mom asked the driver if she could ride along with them to the school. She hadn't planned this but she was very relieved when the driver gave permission, which meant she didn't have to return up the hill with Carla. The two women had never been friends, only short-term neighbors. The tragic accident would leave a rift between them forever. Mom knew she could eventually forgive, but she'd never be able to forget the circumstances of her loss and anguish. Carla had not meant to miss the stop sign, but a child had died because of the error. That fact could never be erased.

As soon as the bus left the children off at the schoolhouse steps, Mom headed for home on foot. She walked quickly because the air was damp and chill and because her nerve endings were sparked as if on fire. Her head and heart throbbed as she fully absorbed the realization that Scotty would never know a first day of school. No special lunch box, no new shoes, no teacher to adore. She was overcome with the unfairness of it all: Carla's children were alive and starting this new beginning while Scotty was dead, buried and deprived of this joy. "He loved school so much," she thought as she wiped away her tears. "He was a little jealous of Phillip going to 'real school' and learning to read ahead of him, but he was so confident that he'd catch up. And he would have been a super star... Oh my God, it's not fair!"

The fog had, in fact, cleared away by the time Mom reached home forty minutes later. Her tears were spent and a few rays of sunshine warmed her back. Heidi wiggled and wagged a greeting that eased her homecoming after a stressful start to the morning. The big house felt especially quiet and empty. As I watched from Heaven I wished I could make a bunch of noise or get her to read me a story that would make us both laugh. I tried with all my might to make the love link so she'd feel my spirit around her. I think it worked because Mom decided to spend the day with things that reminded her of me in happy times.

She took the shovel to plant the potted blue spruce a friend had brought after the memorial service. She chose a place in the yard that was near enough to the house and an electrical outlet so the little tree could be decorated with Christmas lights every winter. Mom and I had spent lots of time working in the yard together. We raked leaves as a family. Phillip and I loved jumping into the piles, burying our bodies while our old dog, Sonya, pawed and dug to find us. Mom decided to "naturalize" our wooded yard with daffodil bulbs from Jackson and Perkins. That meant she'd toss a handful of bulbs in a spray across the yard, then we'd hunt to find them in the tall grass and dig a hole to plant them wherever they landed. I was good at finding the bulbs and could hardly wait until spring when the plants would bloom. I got to see them and pick a bouquet that first spring, but I guessed Phillip would have to be the picker from now on.

In the afternoon Mom took my sandals to a store in town where they put bronze on baby shoes and made them into bookends. My Seattle grandma had asked to take my cowboy boots and make bookends out of them. We had lots of books at our house so I guess Mom could use a couple more sets of bookends.

She had been reading some books about getting over the death of a child. She wanted to keep around enough reminders so that I would never be forgotten by our family, but not so many that it would be morbid and sad. Mom determined to convert the room that had been mine into a guest room that would get some use by company. She thought visitors wouldn't want to sleep in a room decorated for a kid who was dead. The spruce tree in the front yard, the bookends, picture albums, the blue memory box: these would keep people reminded that I am an angel now but my spirit is still with them as they live their lives on Earth.

When Mom walked down to meet Phillip's bus at the end of the school day, she talked with one of the teenage cousins who had been sent to meet Carla's kids. She learned that Carla was planning to move back to Texas as soon as she worked out the details. The doctor had given the okay for the move since they were almost all better from their accident injuries. Mom thought that was a very positive development: a new beginning for Carla's family away from the unhappy memory of the wreck, and a chance for Mom to resume relationships with the neighbors and the school folks without the sadness, jealousy and anger that Carla's presence could evoke.

Phillip chattered non-stop as they walked up the hill. "Mom, there are nine kids in first grade and 23 in our classroom. Paul and Carey are brother and sister. They sit beside me because their last name starts with M. Mrs. Down writes real nice on the board and I can read every word. She already knows all the kids' names by heart. We talked about what we did during the summer. I told them about the accident that killed Scotty. Mrs. Down already knew my brother died. She was real gentle. I think she believes in angels, too. I told them Scotty wasn't wearing his seatbelt, and I showed them the scrape scars on my chest where my seatbelt hurt me. After I was done talking Nancy told us that her dog was hit by a car and died during the summer."

There was some testing planned for later that week. Phillip brought home a permission slip Mom needed to sign. He had a picture he'd colored and Mom made a big deal of it as she posted it on the refrigerator. She had chosen to remove the artwork that I made at Little Beavers in the summertime before I died. It was put away with other treasures in the blue memory box. The refrigerator was going to be dedicated to Phillip from now on. He needed extra attention to help him get beyond the huge tragedy in his young life and to know that he was loved and cherished every bit as much as my memory would be.

16 Life Goes On

Dad had a bad knee that hurt him if he had to stand in the operating room for long hours at a time. He had injured it playing high school football, then it got worse when he skiied or ran as a grown-up. A famous knee surgeon in Eugene had agreed to fix it on September 20. Since all the arrangements had been made for a long time, Mom and Dad decided to go ahead and get the operation over with, even though Dr. Chester advised that they should postpone it until they got over my death. Mom and Dad said, "Well, we can't postpone life. Better to just get on with the plans we've made and work around the disappointments we can't control." Another doctor friend offered his vacation home in Central Oregon so my family would have a relaxing place to rest after the surgery.

Lots of our family friends were figuring out how to be helpful so as to ease the pain and get my parents through the difficult and lonely months ahead. Three of the doctors' wives, Karen, Sandy and Michelle, decided to develop a foursome for doubles tennis at an indoor court in Salem. Mom had been taking tennis lessons in a P.E. course at Oregon State in the months before I died. The four women started playing every week and had some good laughs and exercise. Since Mom was only going to Corvallis a couple days a week for fall term she could do more stuff in Salem with the friends and neighbors around home.

Phillip got signed up for T-ball and soccer after school. He liked sports, especially the uniforms and equipment he wore. His testing from the school showed that he had some "perceptual-motor learning disabilities" that needed special attention, so Mom and Dad worked with the school and a therapist who would come to the classroom to help him. He was the best reader in his class, even counting the second and third graders, but he had trouble writing, using scissors, doing art work...things like that. He seldom came close to hitting the ball off the T, and he shied away from the crowd around the soccer ball, unsure of when to kick and when to just avoid being shoved and falling down.

Mom's class at OSU started at the very end of September. She was able to arrange her schedule so she'd be with Phillip in the morning until his bus time, then be back home when the bus dropped him off in the afternoon. Driving thirty miles back and forth every Tuesday and Thursday was very lonely with no kids along for the ride. She had to pass by the crash site and Little Beavers. That was hard. She considered the advice of friends who thought she should take a totally different route, but that would have meant about 20 extra miles each way and Mom said it was "not practical...a waste of time and gas...just avoiding a situation that was better confronted."

Besides her one class, Mom's big task for fall term was developing a research project for her dissertation. Her faculty committee had already seen a draft of her idea for research about men's and women's roles and some things called "androgyny" and "feminism." Phillip once showed me the pictures with a story he read in TIME magazine about the women's revolution. We giggled about the "bra-burning." Phillip asked Mom if she burned her bras when she was young. "Well, not actually," she said, "but I participated in some anti-war events and some campaigns to get women more rights. Bra-burning was a symbol of some of those peace and justice activities that were common in the years just before you boys were born."

Now Mom was talking to her major professor about changing her research topic to something about grief after a child dies. She was afraid Dr. Wall would deny such a request because it would be hard to do "objective" research, being so personally close to the subject. Dr. Wall was actually encouraging when Mom told her how little she had found in the literature that was helpful for surviving families trying to get through grief work. She told Mom to develop a formal proposal for the committee who had approval and denial powers. Dr. Wall supported Mom in convincing the committee that such research could be a meaningful contribution to the body of knowledge that existed.

Mom's thirty-fifth birthday came on October 6. Dr. Wall and three of Mom's student friends took her out to lunch to celebrate. It wasn't a very good day for Mom but the group was kind and not expecting her to put on a happy face and act as if nothing bad had happened when she was thirty-four. "Frankly," she told them, "I feel as if half my life is over along with half my reason for living." She felt old and depressed. The good part was that they were there for her whether she was cheery and optimistic or not. They gave her two gift certificates, one for the bookstore and one at a lingerie shop in Corvallis.

On the tenth of October Mom decided she felt strong enough to stop by the accident site in Suver. Dad had questioned her need to do this but she told him she needed to get the facts and have all the pieces of the puzzle to understand and process what had happened. The crossroads had buildings on two corners: a small general store and an old-time gas station. Another corner had a stack of about a thousand old car tires. We had passed those tires every day for a year and I had wondered what it would be like to climb up that black rubber mountain. Mom parked in front of the store and went inside where a woman behind the counter greeted her. There were no other customers around so Mom approached the clerk and introduced herself. "My name is Cheron Mayhall. My little boy was killed in the accident here on July 22. I was wondering if you know someone who could tell me about that evening."

The clerk shifted on her feet and turned red in the face. When she got over her shock, she came around and put her hand on Mom's shoulder. "I'm so sorry, Cheron. My heart has felt a bit broken ever since the accident. I was working here when the crash occurred and I ran right outside. I'm a member of the Suver volunteer fire department so I went to work trying to help the poor people in the car. One of the kids in the front seat was crying, but the rest were very quiet." She noticed that Mom's tears had started so she asked, "Are you sure you want to hear the details?" Mom nodded Yes.

"I heard the siren and knew other volunteers would be arriving soon and that someone would have called 9-1-1 for emergency vehicles. We were very scared because the car was smoking and leaking fluid very close to the gas pumps at the station next door. If a fire got started, it could spread to that stack of old tires and cause a huge fire. My buddies and I got the three biggest kids out of the car and laid them carefully on the ground away from the danger of fire. While a couple of the guys worked to get the driver out from under the steering wheel, I cradled Scotty in my arms and sat with him on the steps of the store. I rocked him like my own son and I cried because it looked to me like he was very badly hurt inside. He had trouble breathing and he was totally limp. But he wasn't all beat up or anything. I mean, there wasn't any blood. He looked like an angel in cowboy boots."

Mom wept and the lady joined her with a flood of her own tears. They went arm in arm to the front of the store where the lady sat Mom down on a stool and got two Cokes out of the cooler. Mom thanked her for being so motherly to me on the night of the crash and for explaining what had happened. The ambulances had come from Corvallis and took away all the victims, including the guy who was driving the truck that hit Carla's car broadside. "We helped the highway emergency crew clean up the spill and the police had the two vehicles towed away before dark. I couldn't sleep at all that night, wondering how I would survive if I had been in your shoes, Cheron. I am so very sorry. I'm glad you came by because I have thought of calling you several times. I just didn't know if you would welcome my call and I didn't want to add to your pain."

"I'll be all right," Mom said as she got back into her yellow Mercedes. "It helps me a lot to know the truth rather than to imagine what might have happened. Scotty never regained consciousness and died before he got to the hospital, but at least I know he was in good hands in those final minutes. If I couldn't have been there for him, I'm glad you were. Thank you so much." They held hands for a few additional moments before Mom backed out and headed north for home. She was relieved though exhausted. She said a prayer of thanks to God for giving her the strength to get through this and for the lady who had helped when I was dying. She forced herself to think of me as an angel in Heaven with Jesus.

17 An Afternoon with Jesus

GG said she had an exciting announcement to make after everybody finished dinner and dessert. That night we were having GG's yummy fruit cobbler made with apricots, so most of us kids had to be reminded not to gobble our food or scrape every bit of the sauce from our dessert bowls. Uncle Alex tried to set an example and eat real slow, but I could see he was excited to get through with eating and on to the surprise GG had in store.

"Okay," said GG when Lila finished her last bite and set down her spoon. "While I was at the market today I heard that Jesus is coming our way in just ten days. He wants all the little children to come see Him. Several of you haven't met Jesus yet, but those of us who have met Him know that it will be a very special day."

"Is He coming to our house?" asked Sasha.

"No, no I don't think so," replied GG. "He is asking that children in this part of Heaven meet Him in the meadow beside the ash grove, which is not far from here."

"So, can we walk there or will we be flying by our spirits?" I asked.

"We can do either or both," answered Unk. "If we walk the whole way it'll take half a day, but it's good exercise. It depends on how much stuff we want to take with us and how much energy we'll want to have when we get there."

"I have an idea," said Esther. " How 'bout we spirit our way over the rocky part and then start walking when we get to the soft meadow grass? Last time we went over there I got rocks in my sandals. It bothered me even more when I tried to go barefoot."

"We can save our energy and still arrive at the meeting place on foot," said GG. "Last time we visited Jesus at that spot it was fun to march along the path for about a mile because we could see the crowd gathering in the distance and that was exciting."

"I know what!" cheeped Steve. "We can march while we sing 'Jesus Loves the Little Children.' If anyone doesn't know that song, I can teach it to you. I learned it at Sunday school when I was a kid on Earth."

Half of the kids said they knew the song and everyone thought the one-mile march was a good idea. GG reminded us that we'd be carrying some blankets and snacks so we'd be comfortable sitting on the ground and not get hungry while we listened to Jesus' stories.

"Aren't we going to take some presents to give to Jesus?" I asked. "Remember how the Littlest Angel took presents to the baby Jesus? Would it be okay if we all took a gift, even though it probably isn't Jesus' birthday?"

"That's a grand idea," GG replied. "We have ten days to be thinking of gifts that might be suitable." All the kids shook their heads enthusiastically. I could tell they were already trying to decide what they could offer Jesus the grown-up, who wasn't a baby in a manger anymore.

In the days that followed all of us did some serious thinking so we could offer gifts that would be pleasing in His sight. Steve was the first to announce his decision: he would take his favorite birdhouse, the one he'd made with wood left over from the tree house built in Uncle Bob's back yard. One of the teens had helped him put it together with nails. He painted it light green with a red roof. A mother swallow had nested in it already. Steve had loved seeing how she fed worms and bugs to her babies and taught them to fly. He was looking forward to having the birds come back again in nesting season, but he loved Jesus and thought the birdhouse would make Jesus happy just as it had entertained him. Besides, he had a couple more birdhouses, just not as pretty as this one.

Freddy, Nathan and Samuel had a pow-wow and decided they wanted to catch some bugs and make a little bug town in a big glass jar. They found an old bird's nest, some soft moss and some twigs of golden wheat which they arranged in the jar. They planned to wait to catch the bugs on the morning before the trip to see Jesus so that the ladybugs, fireflies and butterflies they captured wouldn't be stuck in the jar for too long. They decided they'd ask Jesus to unscrew the lid and set the bugs free so that all who were there could enjoy seeing them fly away. It would be sort of like the fireworks at the end of the Fourth of July picnic back in the United States.

Osmin and Sasha loved to help with the baking in GG's kitchen, so they decided to make a big batch of hot-cross buns for Jesus. GG suggested a double batch so our family could taste-test some of the buns before they wrapped the rest in a colorful basket with a ribbon on the handle.

Esther and Lila loved all the flowers in Heaven. They decided to weave a beautiful necklace of tiny lawn daisies. Lila remembered how the hula ladies had put flower necklaces over the heads of all her family when they'd been on vacation in Hawaii. This memory made her feel a little lonely for her parents and sisters, but she recalled how sweet the flowers smelled and how everyone became real friendly and kissed each other on the cheeks. Esther wondered if they were supposed to kiss Jesus when they gave Him the daisy-chain necklace. Lila said they could play it by ear and see how much kissing was going on in the crowd around Jesus.

Jesus (the kid) and Gilberto were best pals and roommates at GG's. They had often discussed what they knew about Jesus, the Son of God. They could recall the Bible stories better than the rest of us and they could recite all sorts of prayers by heart. Both of them had strings of beads they called rosaries. It took them about six days to come up with a good idea for a gift. They asked GG and Unk if it would be okay to wash and dry Jesus' feet, like He and His disciples did for one another. GG helped them find a little basin, a small cup of soap, and a soft, blue towel. Gilberto had been on the path to the ash grove before so he knew there was a stream where they could fill the basin with cool water before arriving for story time.

Heather wanted to give Jesus some of her favorite barrettes and scrunchies. She remembered the pictures of Jesus in storybooks and on the stained-glass window behind the altar of her family's church. He had long, beautiful hair. She wished her own hair was like Jesus' instead of curly and red. Finally she decided to take the hair-do things in her pocket until she knew if it was a good gift. She also decided to practice a song she could sing especially for Jesus. She remembered the one about Zacchaeus, the wee little man who sat up in the sycamore tree until Jesus told him to come down. Heather had a sweet voice and I knew Jesus would like her song.

I checked through all my earthly toys and equipment but nothing seemed like a good Jesus gift, now that Jesus was all grown up. It wasn't until three days before the trip to the ash grove that I had a great idea: I would make Him a walking stick. When we hiked as a family on Earth, Mommy always liked to find a strong stick to help her walk or to point out things along the path. I asked Uncle Bob and Uncle Alex if I could get a piece of a branch from either the treehouse maple or the chestnut tree. They asked one of the teens named Joshua to cut a good branch for me. I peeled the bark, smoothed the knobs where twigs had branched off, and rubbed the stick with sand and GG's cooking oil so it was shiny and you couldn't get slivers from it.

When the big day came we all gathered on GG's front porch with our gifts and supplies for the day. It was the most exciting day I'd had in Heaven, so far. GG was carrying the three blankets we'd be sitting on. She would be leading our group, while Unk would bring up the rear carrying a picnic basket with bread and fruit for snacking. We all held our gifts tight as we spirited our way toward the ash grove. Uncle Bob and Mrs. Wettleson waved and smiled as we departed. About a mile short of our destination we began our walk along the path. Actually, we marched as Steve led us in singing "Jesus Loves the Little Children, All the Children of the World." We had to sing it faster and faster as we kept marching faster and faster, eager to join the crowd of kids we could see gathering beneath the shade of the trees. We went over a little stream where Gilberto and Jesus stooped to fill their foot-washing basin with cool water.

GG studied the forming audience and spied a little knoll where we might perch so we could see Jesus over the crowd. It looked to me like there were about thirty kids by the time everyone had arrived. Jesus had come with another angel-person who wore a furry outfit. He looked like a caveman — like Fred Flintstone. They walked into the center of the crowd so they could be as close as possible to all the children. The other guy was carrying a chunk of tree trunk. He set it on the ground in the middle of the circle and Jesus, the Son of God, stepped on top of it so everyone could see him better.

Jesus was wearing a long white dress and sandals, just like the pictures I'd seen of Him. His hair was short and curly like Heather's, but it was dark brown instead of red. I looked over at Heather and saw that she was practicing her song, realizing that the barrettes and scrunchies weren't going to work for Jesus. Jesus did not have a backpack or anything to carry His storybooks. I guessed He was even a better storyteller than Uncle Alex since he'd been going around doing it since Bible times. As Jesus got ready to speak, GG asked us all to hold hands so we could remind each other with a little squeeze that we needed to be good, quiet listeners.

Jesus' voice was strong and I could hear every word as He introduced the other man as his cousin, John. He told us about how John's parents, Elizabeth and Zechariah, were married a long time without having children, though they prayed about it every day. Finally God sent an angel to tell Zech that they would have a baby and they should name him John. The idea made Zech happy, but he didn't really believe the angel so the angel told him he would be unable to speak until the baby was born. Sure enough, a baby came along and all their friends came by their house asking, "What are you going to name him?" Zech still couldn't talk, so Elizabeth said, "John." The friends said they ought to name him Zechariah like his dad and granddaddy. Zech wrote a note in big letters saying, "His name is John!" After that Zechariah could speak again. His first words were probably, "Thank you, God, for giving me back my voice!"

The second part of the John story was about when he was a grown-up on Earth. Jesus told us that His cousin lived in the wilderness. It made me think of Davy Crockett who was "raised in the woods where he knew every tree, kilt him a bar when he was only three." John liked to wear animal skins and he ate little bugs and plants that grew around the desert where he lived. God took good care of John and led him to be a preacher and to baptize people. When he was about thirty years old he got a chance to baptize his own cousin, Jesus. He didn't just sprinkle water on peoples' heads, he took them into the river and dunked them! Anyhow, right after Jesus' dunking the sky opened up and God spoke from Heaven to tell everyone that Jesus was His own special Son. I started to raise my hand because I wanted to tell Jesus and John about all my cousins, but Steve gave it a little squeeze and I remembered GG had told us not to interrupt.

Because I love zoo animals and rainbows, my favorite story that day was about Noah and the flood. Jesus was such a good storyteller I could close my eyes and see the huge ark and all the animals, two-by-two. His voice grew louder when He told us about the thunder and lightning. I could remember sometimes in Salem when the rain pounded down on our roof and the driveway flooded. I remembered about the doves and the olive branches, and how the ark ended up stuck on a mountain when the flood waters dried up. Nathan, who was holding my other hand, leaned over and whispered, "I remember when we had a big flood in Missouri. We built a wall out of sandbags across our front yard. Our puppy ran away while we were busy, and we never saw him again." I whispered back, "Sorry, Nate."

When Jesus started telling a story about a little boy named Samuel, all us kids looked over at OUR Samuel. He was beaming; we could tell he had heard the story about his name before. This was another Bible story about a man and his wife who really wanted a baby. Finally God answered their prayers and Samuel was born. Jesus told us that an old priest named Eli asked the parents if they'd let Samuel come live with the leaders in the temple where he could learn about God faster. Little Sam woke up three nights in a row when he thought he heard Eli calling to him. But Eli said, "No, I didn't call you." After this kept happening, Eli realized it was God's voice that Sam heard so he told him to listen carefully to whatever God was saying. God told Samuel He would guide him to be a leader of the people, what they call a prophet. That's how Samuel became a famous Bible character.

The last story Jesus told was about one of His own miracles. It happened one day when He was telling stories to a big crowd of people, lots more than the kids at the ash grove that afternoon. Jesus saw that the people were looking tired and hungry. They must have forgotten to bring snacks. He asked his friends, Philip and Andrew, where they could buy food, but they said it was too expensive and there wasn't a market nearby. Andrew had noticed a young boy in the audience with a basket of brown bread and a couple of silver fish. Jesus called the kid forward and they agreed to share this food with all the hungry people. The amazing thing was that just five loaves of bread and two small fish, which were blessed by Jesus, turned out to be plenty of food for the whole crowd!

That gave Osmin and Sasha a bright idea. They scampered over to where GG was sitting on the grass. "Can we ask Jesus to make our hot-cross buns into a snack for all the kids?"

GG could see that Jesus was ready to stop His storytelling and just chat for awhile, so she agreed with the plan. Osmin and Sasha said "excuse me" as they made their way through the crowd to where Jesus now sat. They knelt down before Jesus and His cousin, John, and said, "Lord Jesus, we have brought a basket of buns we made in GG's kitchen yesterday. We are wondering if you could make a miracle so all the people here can have a taste."

Jesus' smile was warm and His dark brown eyes sparkled. "You are most generous, boys. Let me have the beautiful basket you have brought." He looked inside at the hot-cross buns and his smile widened. As he bowed his head, everyone else took a hint and did the same. "Heavenly Father, we ask your blessings on this food and on all the precious children in Heaven and on Earth. Bless these hot-cross buns for our enjoyment and nourishment. Amen."

The crowd that had been so quiet now broke into happy noises as Jesus and John handed out one plump bun to each child, and the grown-ups, too. There was laughter and some lip-smacking as the sweet frosting and raisins brought pleasure to the hungry people. Sasha and Osmin were the happiest children in the ash grove, seeing that their gift for Jesus was multiplied and being enjoyed by all.

Jesus invited every one of the children to come to Him. Those up front got there first. GG reminded us to be patient and mind our manners, but it was hard. A few other kids had brought gifts for Jesus, too, but I was too short and couldn't see what they were. Uncle Alex lifted up Esther and Lila, one on each of his shoulders. They told us how Jesus touched and blessed all the boys and girls, one by one.

When our turn finally came, Jesus hadn't become tired at all. He paid attention to each of us and acted like our gifts were just what He always wanted. Esther and Lila knelt for a second, then asked the Lord Jesus to bend down so they could slip the necklace of daisies onto His shoulders. He put one of His hands on each of their heads to bless them, then He hugged them to His chest. They couldn't help hugging back and kissing His cheeks.

Heather came forward next, singing her song about the wee little man. She sang it over several times because it seemed to bring such pleasure to Jesus and John. Steve and I could see there were still lots of kids waiting their turns to touch Jesus, so we brought our gifts forward even before Heather's singing stopped. Jesus drew us close to Him and said, "You boys have done well with the works of your hands. Steve, I will remember you every time I see the nesting birds and hear their chirpping or singing."

I especially remember His kind words about the walking stick I'd made. "Scotty," said Jesus, as he admired it's varied wood colors and smooth surface, "this stick is a symbol of love and comfort. I remember, on the morning after you died in the accident, your mother read the Twenty-third Psalm from her Bible. The words promise that the Lord God will always care for His beloved people. Even when they 'walk through the valley of the shadow of death' they can depend on God's loving guidance. 'Thy rod and staff they comfort me.' This walking stick is a 'rod' and a 'staff' of comfort. I will use it to strengthen and guide my steps as I journey now and forever with you and your family. The love you have given and received during your earthly life will never cease and always be treasured. It is now expanded to the realms of angels, interconnected with the eternal love God promises to all."

Jesus handed our gifts to John so he could take us into His lap. When He hugged me it was the warmest feeling I ever had, even better than hugs from my mom and dad. Heather had finished her song so she squeezed between me and Steve so that Jesus was hugging all three of us at once.

The remaining boys in our group had decided that Gilberto and Jesus should wash and dry Jesus' feet – John's feet, too – before the rest handed over the bug garden in a jar. I could see from the look on Jesus' face that he was refreshed by the cool water on his feet. He invited cousin John to sit beside him on the stump so each of the boys had a pair of tired, dirty feet to work on. While His feet were being dried with the towel, the Lord laid His hands on the heads of Gilberto and Jesus. I felt warm all over again as He gave them His blessings.

Unk smiled and nodded to Freddy, Nathan and Samuel who had been waiting their turn. They pushed and shoved just a little because all three wanted to have their hands on the bug jar as they approached Jesus. Jesus put his finger in front of His lips to quiet the crowd so everyone could hear the chirpping and buzzing coming from the jar. The boys had found a few crickets and a honey bee, in addition to the fireflies, ladybugs and butterflies they caught early in the day. Samuel introduced himself and thanked Jesus for telling the story about the prophet named Samuel, then he told the Lord of their idea to let all the bugs go free. Jesus held the jar up above His head for all to see, then He unscrewed the lid. The flying insects caught a gentle breeze as they escaped back into God's creation where they belonged. All the people said "Oh" and "Ah," mixed with giggles of delight, as the beautiful bugs rose into the air. Then Jesus laid the jar beside Him on the ground so the crickets could scamper away and hide themselves in the deep grass. The boys felt happy and blessed even before He laid His hands on each of their heads.

By the time Jesus finished attending to every child it was becoming dark. GG and Unk called a pow-wow and thanked us for being so well-behaved all afternoon. We waved to Jesus and John as our spirits whisked us away toward GG's house. I knew this was going to be one of my best memories ever. Steve and I would have a lot to talk about for many nights to come before we fell asleep.

18 Dreams, Images, Searching for Answers

Mom dreamt about me many nights, but usually couldn't remember any details when she woke up. Some mornings she didn't want to wake up or get out of bed because it meant facing the hard reality of me being dead. In her dreams we were together or I was somewhere happy, but in waking I was dead and gone and she was lonely and unhappy.

One night her dream was so real she got up and wrote it down. She had seen me strolling down a pathway among clouds in Heaven with a big white goose under my arm. I was laughing and talking with my friend, Adrian, who was on his tricycle beside me. It didn't make much sense because Adrian was alive and well, but the dream lifted Mom's spirits because I seemed so happy. Later she figured out that the goose was probably an image from the front cover of Phillip's favorite Mother Goose book which Mom had replaced on the shelf just before going to bed. It made me wonder if Mom remembered the goose that ate her buttons at GG's farm when she was a little girl, or if she had an inkling about the geese in our heavenly back yard!

Dad took Mom and Phillip to see the movie, "Close Encounters of the Third Kind" starring Richard Dreyfuss. Of course, I was watching them from Heaven above so I got to see the movie too. It was the best, most grown-up movie I ever saw. One of the stars was a little blonde boy about four years old. The story was about spaceships and friendly aliens that stole the boy from Earth. His mom was so scared because she thought she'd never see him again. But Richard Dreyfuss kept trying to figure out the sounds the alien ships were making and the code to discover where they planned to land when they came to Earth the next time. Most people thought he was nuts, but the little boy's mother stood by him and they ended up going to Devil's Tower in Wyoming. It turns out this guy was right and pretty soon the spaceship landed, the door opened and creatures started walking down the ramp.

Mom grabbed Dad's arm and held Phillip's hand when the little blonde boy came through the spooky smoke and walked back onto the Earth. Mom was so shocked she felt limp and the tears poured down her cheeks like a waterfall. She probably felt joy like the mom in the movie who was desperate for her son to come back, but then she realized the kid was just an actor and the movie story wasn't real. It took awhile to catch her breath so she could stand up when the lights came on. She told Phillip and Dad about the feelings she was having and they were spooked a little bit too. They all wondered if it was a sign that I was at least doing okay, even if I wasn't going to be arriving back on a spaceship in Wyoming.

Things like this happened all the time for Mom. She had lots of hours alone at home since Phillip was in school all day, Dad was at work, and she only went to college a couple times a week. She tried to read a lot of inspirational books and find fun things to do because having idle hours made her feel very old and lonely. Sometimes she got angry with people who seemed to carry on with a matter-of-fact attitude and wanted her to get over it and act the same as she did before I died. "Put 'em in the ground and get on with life..." was what they seemed to be saying. It made her mad. Life was out of kilter, she told my dad, and she couldn't seem to find a balance without more answers. Why did Scotty have to die? Where is Scotty's spirit now? How do we keep him in our hearts forever without feeling the chest pain and emptiness?

Abraham Lincoln was one of Mom's heros, right up there with Albert Schweitzer (which reminded me I should ask GG if she'd seen Abe around Heaven). In one of her books of quotes she found some comforting words spoken by President Lincoln. Two of his own sons died, and he grieved for all the "sons" who died in the Civil War.

> In this sad world of ours sorrow comes to all...It
> comes with bitterest agony...Perfect relief is not

> possible. Except with time. You cannot now realize that you will ever feel better. And yet, this is a mistake. You are sure to be happy again. To know this, which is certainly true, will make you some less miserable now. I have had experience enough to know what I say.

It wasn't easy to find helpful words written by parents after their child had died. That's what Mom needed most and why she was planning to interview and study these families for her college research paper. She remembered the book *Death Be Not Proud*, by John Gunther, which she'd read in high school. It belonged to her teacher, Mr. Wettleson, who was now the heavenly neighbor I called Uncle Bob. Mr. and Mrs. Gunther's boy got real sick and died. They wrote a book all about it. The mom, Frances Gunther, talked about feeling guilty:

> I think every parent must have a sense of failure, even of sin, merely in remaining alive after the death of a child. One feels that it is not right to live when one's child has died, that one should somehow have found the way to give one's life to save his life. Failing there, one's failures during his too brief life seem all the harder to bear and forgive.

This mom, Frances, eventually figured out some answers and a plan of action that made sense for her so she could go on living. She wondered, "How can we make up for the lost opportunity to have loved our child more? What does it mean now – to love him more?"

> To me, it means loving life more, being more aware of life, of one's fellow human beings, of the earth. It means obliterating, in a curious but real way, the ideas of evil and hate and the enemy, and transmuting them, with the alchemy of suffering, into

ideas of clarity and charity. It means caring more and more about other people, at home and abroad, all over the earth. It means caring more about God. I hope we can love our son more and more until we die, and leave behind us, as he did, the love of love, the love of life.

All that made sense to Mom and seemed to give her hope. It was the kind of stuff she'd learned at church – keep loving and caring and trusting no matter what happens. It still didn't make sense for little children to die. One day when our neighbor, Gramma Edna, was visiting, she told Mom, "We can find strength in knowing that God doesn't make mistakes." She had lost a child, too, and had found comfort in that belief. It didn't work so well for Mom though. She wrote a journal entry about it:

> I can't help thinking it WAS a mistake – not planned. Not that I hold God responsible. I believe Scotty died due to man's fallibility and negligence. God IS the master planner, and I find some solace in believing the plan includes something beyond this earthly life, especially for the little ones whose time here is cut so short. But I don't believe that God either caused or might have prevented this auto accident. The part God plays in this incident can be perceived in the spirit of love that prevails beyond death and loss – the spirit that bolsters us enough to go on searching for new sources of hope and joy. My faith in the healing power of the Spirit of Love gives me assurance that Bill and I will be happy again, someday.
> – Cheron, October 22, 1977

Mom told Gramma Edna, "I think part of what makes it so hard is that I'm such a planner. I had planned having all our children before I was thirty so they'd be grown up by the time Bill and I were fifty. We'd be young enough to keep up with them, and probably have some healthy years to enjoy grandchildren, too. I figured I'd get out of graduate school in a couple years and have a career as a counselor throughout the years of parenting my school-age children. With Scotty's death, I've lost a sense of order in my life. I don't know what to expect anymore.

"I don't think I'm a control freak or inflexible, but losing a child defies the natural order of life. We never expect to outlive our children, do we? Before Scotty's death, life seemed orderly; after Scotty's death, life seems chaotic. What I've been realizing is how much parents tend to invest their hope for the future in their children. Without hope, or with that hope greatly diminished, it's hard to go on from day to day and to plan for the future with any certainty."

Gramma Edna remembered the chaos after child loss but couldn't recall feeling such a loss of hope. "Have faith that God will restore your strength and hope," she told Mom. Just the fact that Gramma Edna had lost a baby and was now leading a happy life was comforting and encouraging. Several women came forward during those first few months to tell Mom they'd survived losing a child. They told her life became good again after a while. Phillip had some wise words to add one day after school when he found Mom crying in the kitchen while fixing supper. "Don't you think Scotty is one of God's angels? Don't be so sad, Mom. He's in a happy, beautiful place."

One evening Mom and Dad were reviewing the long days since the accident. They both agreed that their defenses were down and they weren't able to concentrate and perform as efficiently as before. "It used to be so much easier to handle the little problems as they arose. Now every bad happening seems like a monstrous insult." During the trip to Texas they had had problems with the rental car. The airline lost some luggage. Mom lost the camera. After they were back home Mom noticed one day that the diamond was gone from her engagement ring. Then a neighbor's car hit

Heidi on the road in front of our house and she had to be patched up by the vet. To top it off, both Mom and Dad felt really upset and helpless when they decided to explore adopting another child but the adoption agencies discouraged them.

At first Mom was shocked when some people suggested, "Have another baby…adopt a child." She was angry because they seemed to imply that my dying was not such a big deal and I could be replaced with another child. It took some hard thinking to accept the fact that the void left after I was killed would always be there. Some hope and joy was definitely lost forever, but she came around to realizing that she needed to keep searching for happiness and that adding a new child to the family might help.

Mom told Satsuki, her best friend at college, she felt odd…like she had "Bereaved Parent" written across her forehead for everyone to see. She had also noticed how she organized time and events according to B.D., before death, and A.D., after death. If someone mentioned a vacation, Mom would say, "Oh, you were in New York the week before Scotty died." Or when my Granny from Seattle complimented Mom on her new hairstyle she had replied, "I got it cut about six weeks after Scotty was killed." She felt weird about these things and hoped they would change. Maybe adopting another child would help to lift her from this emphasis on death and grief.

Mom and Dad made appointments at two state-run adoption agencies. They filled out tons of paperwork and met with counselors to discuss the process. They said they'd prefer a child under three years old. They would be willing and able to take a boy or girl who had trouble walking or things like that because Dad knew how to take care of such problems. At both agencies the counselors were very discouraging because they didn't think my parents had gotten over their grief well enough yet. Mom tried to reason with them: "We are in our mid-thirties, we are both in the helping professions, we know about managing pain and sorrow, we have experience raising children, we know the adoption process will likely take more than a year..." Still, the agencies told them they'd keep the forms on file and maybe call them in a year or two.

By late-October the only agency that was encouraging was the Holt International Adoption Program in Eugene, Oregon. Holt helped families adopt children from other countries like China or Korea. They told my folks to fill out all the paperwork and that they seemed like good candidates to adopt within a year or so. That's when Dad told Mom he'd been talking with his friend who was a urology doctor. They'd discussed an operation to reverse Dad's vasectomy so he could try to make another baby. It was a new kind of operation and the doctor told Dad he'd had fifty percent success. He'd done it twice and one of the couples had made a baby and the other hadn't! Dad decided to schedule the surgery for Thanksgiving vacation so he and Mom could try to make a baby while they were waiting to see if Holt could find a child for them.

19 Praying for Babies

One night before bed, I told my heavenly roommate, Steve, all about how my parents were wanting to get another child. "Do you mean they want to let another kid use your room and your toys?" he asked. "Is that okay with you?"

"Well," I told him, "angels in Heaven must not get jealous because it doesn't bother me at all. Maybe I would be upset if I was down on Earth, but from here it seems like a wonderful idea. I heard Phillip telling his friends he wants to be a big brother again. I'm sure getting a new kid would make my parents happier. I'm never going to get back there to use my stuff and sleep in that bed Granddaddy made for me."

Steve thought a long time about his own family on Earth. He was his parents' first baby, but they had two girl babies join the family before Steve got sick and died. Now his two sisters were going to school, but he knew his mom and dad felt sad because they did not have a boy. "I have a good idea," he said. "Why don't we pray real hard every night so God can make a miracle and get babies for our families on Earth?"

"Hey," I said, "remember how God helped Abraham and Sarah get a baby even when they were very old? And remember Samuel in the story Jesus told the other day? His parents were very old too, but God finally helped them make a baby boy. Let's pray with all our might and see what God can do about getting babies for our families."

"C'mon, get down on your knees." We bowed our heads, folded our hands together, and rested our elbows on the bed as Steve prayed. "God, you have lots more power than Superman. The Bible says that you make all the people, and we need to order a couple of new little people to help our Earth families be happier. Could you make a boy baby for my folks? Scotty's folks aren't that particular, so just find them a good baby. It doesn't matter what color or anything. Maybe they'd like two new kids, so you could make a couple of different kinds for their family. You're gonna be hearing this prayer every night until you make these miracles happen. Thanks for listening. Oh, and thank you God for being our Heavenly Father and taking care of us all the time. Amen."

20 Autumn and Halloween

Phillip was very excited as Halloween approached. At school they were planning a big party and he wanted to trick-or-treat with his new friends, Paul and Carey. Carey had a costume of Winnie the Pooh so Phillip decided he wanted to be Tigger. Mom hadn't had time to do much sewing since starting back to college, but now she had extra hours during the day and she enjoyed working with the orange and black striped flannel. Paul was shy about dressing up and being noticed so he was happy to go as the boy, Christopher Robin, dressed in his favorite school outfit.

Uncle Alex and I viewed the preparation for Halloween 1977 and shared memories from a year earlier. Unk had been getting sicker and sicker in Seattle. Granny and Auntie Alice had been so worried and they were exhausted taking him to frequent medical appointments or being at his bedside to help and comfort his wife and kids. Unk encouraged them to take a break. It was decided they'd go spend the weekend prior to Halloween at our house in Oregon. The teenagers at our church made a haunted house to earn money for charity and they threw a big party for the little kids. Auntie Alice told Mom she'd help us find costumes since we'd been driving back and forth to Little Beavers and college everyday and hadn't had time to prepare for Halloween.

Auntie Alice was joyful and funny and she had lots of experience raising boys. For seven years of Halloweens she had dressed and performed as a witch at her sons' schools. She loved being the class mother and had happily volunteered to serve in that role for all the years since her twins started first grade. Now she was class mom for her youngest boy, Darren Kelly. Early on Saturday morning she woke me and Phillip up with her witch's cackle and told us to get dressed so we could get down to the Goodwill store before all the best costumes were sold. Phillip begged to be Dracula because I wanted to be Frankenstein. This was nothing new for Auntie Alice who had dressed David and Daniel as these monsters when they were in second grade.

We had no trouble finding black pants for both of us. Mom found a little black jacket that fit me except for the sleeves being too short. When Auntie Alice stuck a stick across the shoulders to make me look hunch-backed, the sleeves were even shorter. Goodwill also had monster make-up, fake teeth and fangs, and suction-cup bolts that looked like they were screwed into my head and neck. Mom had some black fabric to make a Dracula cape for Phillip and some black yarn she sewed into a shaggy wig for me. Darren Kelly had very long eyelashes and wasn't at all embarrassed about dressing up and going to the church party as a girl. We called him Dee.

Granny dressed as Mother Nature and Mom attached some paper plates and silverware to a big tablecloth she wore like a shawl, strapped a pot of flowers on her head, and went as a table.

Uncle Alex laughed out loud as he remembered our costumes. Of course, he had been home in his special electric hospital bed so he didn't see all of us at the pre-Halloween party, but by the end of that week on the real Halloween night his cancer had done him in and he was already in Heaven with a great view of trick-or-treaters. "What I remember most," he chuckled, "was your excitement telling everyone that you two were 'Fwank' and 'Dwack.' You couldn't pronounce the letter 'r' so those two names came out sounding hilarious. People got such a kick out of it they usually asked you to say it over again. They were so amused and entertained they even gave you a double helping of goodies."

"But," I asked him, "I don't talk funny anymore, do I, Unk? I must'a learned to say my r's about the same time I learned to read, back on the first day I got to Heaven. Remember that day when I met all the kids at GG's house?"

Unk said he remembered it well, but right then he was noticing Mom back on Earth with her memories of my last Halloween. She was smiling and crying at the same time. She stood up from her sewing machine where she was making Phillip's Tigger costume and went to the shelf of photo albums. Sure enough, there were funny pictures of all of us...Fwank, Dwack, Wicked Witch, Dee, Mother Nature and Mom, the Table.

"The people we've left behind have to find a balance between sorrowful memories and joyful memories, and it's never easy," Unk told me. "Right now our family is feeling a double whammy because it's the first anniversary of my death and your death is even more recent. My own kids are too old to trick-or-treat, but they are going to a teen Halloween party and that'll keep them from thinking about me and how they felt when I died a year ago. That's good. Your mom will feel more joy than sadness next Halloween, I'm sure of it. It just takes time for lonely hearts to heal."

Halloween wasn't the only thing about this time of year that made Mom cry about missing me. On the pages of the picture album she saw the photo of Phillip and me in our red sweaters, and Mom in her overalls, raking a huge pile of autumn leaves in our front yard. She convinced Dad to come out and pose with us so this could be our Christmas card picture. We sent out about a hundred cards every year so all our friends who never visited our new place in Salem could see our house and yard in the forest. Dad really hated this picture posing and wouldn't dress up. He just showed up in his regular clothes and couldn't wait until our neighbor, Grampa Larry, snapped enough shots to satisfy Mom. We all smiled – even our Husky dog, Sonya – but Dad usually ended up looking bah-humbug on our Christmas card.

I was aware that Mom was reminiscing about how I helped her plant a hundred daffodil bulbs that last October when we "naturalized. " It had taken a long time to plant one hundred bulbs, but Mom said we'd be proud of our beautiful yard in the springtime. I was already proud because Mom told me what a hard worker and good helper I was. And, sure enough, we had scads of daffodils blooming all over the place by the time I was four the next March. Mom let me pick two bouquets, one for Gramma Edna next door and one for our dining room table.

Another yard chore I did with Mom was gathering cones that had fallen from the Douglas fir trees. Her college friend who lived in New Hampshire was an artist and she made beautiful door wreaths from cones. Every year she sent us one for Christmas. This friend, Elizabeth, had grown up in Portland and she especially loved Douglas fir cones, which didn't grow in the northeast. She said they looked like they had little tongues sticking out all over. One of the things I liked best about getting sacks of cones was the money! I'd been talking to Mom about getting some of my own money to save in my bunny bank or to buy things like toys and Christmas presents. She said she'd give me a penny for every cone I found, as long as it wasn't old and dirty. I earned over two dollars in one weekend.

Phillip didn't like to do jobs like this, but I loved it. I remember when summer came and I asked Mom how I could earn more money. She thought and thought, then suggested I help with the yard work by picking all the yellow dandelions before they made those fluffy round heads that blow apart. She told me the flying seeds were called "wiggies," but later she admitted it was just a word she and her sisters made up when they were kids. Anyhow, I picked a big bag full of dandelions, then Mom and I counted them in piles of ten. The sun was hot and my hands got gooey from the dandelion juice. Pine cones were cleaner and easier so I quit before I got two dollars worth of dandelions. Just the same, I added 177 pennies to my bunny bank. It was so heavy I had a hard time lifting it onto the shelf.

When Dad got home from work that night before Halloweeen in 1977, Mom told him about her memories of the monster costumes, leaf raking for the Christmas picture, planting daffodils, gathering cones and picking dandelions. Dad listened carefully, then said wistfully, "Scotty was so industrious and thrifty. He was always wanting to save money and willing to work for it. Remember when we went on vacation to Wyoming? He was desperate to have that red, white and blue suede wallet in the souvenir store. Said he needed a place to carry his money, 'like Dad.' If he didn't have a pocket in his pants, he'd attach it to his belt alongside his ropes and the little guns or knives he fashioned out of sticks. I bet if he'd lived he'd have grown up into quite the businessman." Dad got a smile out of Mom as they remembered these things together and she imagined me dressed in a business suit with a briefcase and big eyeglasses.

As we witnessed these scenes from Heaven, Uncle Alex put his arm around my shoulder. "The memories are beginning to bring more smiles than tears some days, Scotty. You brought so much happiness to their lives while you were all together that your parents and Phillip can't help but feel warmth and joy in remembering.

They'll get happy again, slowly but surely, you'll see. I'll tell you what: we have leaves from the maple and chestnut trees falling all over GG's yard and Uncle Bob's yard. Why don't you and I organize a work party and do some raking right here? You've noticed we don't have money in Heaven so you won't be getting paid, but I think it'll be fun and we can surprise Uncle Bob and GG."

"Good idea, Unk. We can invite the little kids and the teenagers who aren't too bossy. If we get really big leaf piles we can make a game of running and jumping into them." Steve, Freddy, Nathan and Samuel all wanted to help, but the girls were in the kitchen baking with GG and didn't want to get dirty doing yard work. Two of the big kids from Uncle Bob's house, Amilie and Berta, pitched right in. In no time we had all the raking done, both in the front yards and under the treehouse out back. GG and Heather brought out a plate of warm ginger cookies to thank us for doing a good job. Helen, Uncle Bob's wife, made fruit punch. It was a fun party and I didn't mind doing the work for free. Heck, I couldn't think of a single thing I would have wanted to buy now that I was settled in Heaven, and I'd lost interest in banking pennies. Guess I'd outgrown it.

21 Uncle Bob and Mom

Uncle Bob helped us dump the last of the leaves into GG's compost pile, then he took me up on his shoulders and we headed for the treehouse. He was pretty tall so I didn't have to climb much of the rope ladder before reaching the knotty pine platform. "Looks like all the other kids have headed back inside," Uncle Bob remarked. This time he was wearing Indian moccasins instead of his cowboy boots. He sat Indian style on the floor and I told him about the small beaded moccasins I wore as booties when I was a baby. Actually, I couldn't remember wearing them, but Mom said they'd been a gift from our special friends, Lani and Ted, when I was born. She put them with other keepsakes in a shadow box that hung in our rec room.

"I remember getting your birth announcement in the mail, Scotty," said Uncle Bob. "Your Mom made each announcement by hand. She drew a sketch of Phillip and your Husky dog pulling a baby in a little red wagon labeled 'Mayhall Express.' Helen and I were tickled for your family and so pleased your mom was still corresponding with her 'ole high school teachers. The last time we'd seen her was in Ohio. The school had sent me on sort of a 'forced sabbatical' trip. It was a very stressful time in our lives that took a terrible toll on my health. But the travel with my lovely wife was a good tonic, and we made a point of visiting some of our favorite Franklin graduates along the way."

"How come my mom was in Ohio? Where's Ohio? What's a sabbatical? Were you in trouble with your boss again for throwing books?" I asked.

Uncle Bob invited me to sit cross-legged in front of him as he tried to answer all my questions. It was neat having someone to tell me about my mom, back before I remembered knowing her. "Well, Cheron went to graduate school in Ohio after she got out of the Peace Corps. Several of my top-notch journalism students joined the Peace Corps after college, then most of them scattered to do graduate work at good universities across the country. I was honored that they'd kept in touch through letters. They often dropped by the high school to see us when they were in Seattle. I could tell they'd all been 'infected' with the Albert Schweitzer bug I'd let loose! Most of them were training to be people helpers: teachers, social workers, doctors. They had lofty ambitions and goals," he observed with a far-away look in his eyes. I think I saw a tear. "They just kept making me proud as they grew into adult leaders.

"Helen and I liked to mentor the students who showed a lot of promise but needed someone to champion them. Your mom had her brother, Alex, and two sisters in high school ahead of her. There was another sister in grade school and no dad at home to help raise the family. Did your Uncle Alex tell you he was quite the rascal, getting into trouble and making some bad grades in high school? He really struggled, but the basketball coach didn't give up on him and he finally got through with a diploma, eventually growing into a very fine man. He's been a jewel helping with the kids at our house and GG's. However, some of the faculty at Franklin thought of Alex as a juvenile delinquent – a bad person – and that reflected on his younger sisters. I had only Cheron in classes I taught, but I could see she was an excellent student. It really annoyed me to see all the kids in the family being lumped together based on Alex's reputation. I put in a good word for Cheron whenever I could.

"When she was a junior she excelled in biology and journalism. Both the biology teacher and I tried to get her to specialize and take more coursework and activities with us. But Cheron also loved speech and drama so she divided her time and spent lots of extracurricular hours acting and directing plays. She was good at it, even though she was a bit shy. Helen and I couldn't help but beam with pride when she won the gold medal for her monologue performance in the Walter Reseburg Speech Contest. She performed as the mother of a young man killed in the war, part of a famous play called *All My Sons*. I know your family was proud of her, too, but they couldn't afford flowers. Helen and I bought her a huge bouquet for when the winners were announced. We signed the card 'from your Secret Admirer.' I don't think she ever figured out who sent them, but she told me how thrilled she was."

"Maybe she could'a been a great actress in the movies," I suggested. I remembered how Mom liked to make speeches in church and tell stories in front of an audience.

"Well," continued Uncle Bob, "Cheron finally decided she would be a journalism major in college, which pleased me no end. She was chosen to be a graduation speaker because she was near the top of her high school class. She did a dramatic reading of a poem by Robert Frost with the Franklin choir singing back-up. Again, Helen and I could not have been prouder if she'd been our own daughter. When colleges recruited her I was happy to write letters of recommendation and tried to help her get scholarships. She was the first person in her family to go to college. And, imagine, now she is going to college to study for her Ph.D."

"Oh," I said, not really understanding what Ph.D. meant, "and she went to college in Ohio where you visited her because you were in trouble with the principal. Was that the last time you saw my mom?"

" I believe so," said Uncle Bob. "Shortly after that she met your dad and they got married and moved to Texas. She continued writing her wonderful letters to us, now and then, so we knew she got a good job as a medical social worker, for which she trained in the Peace Corps and in Ohio. She wrote and edited a newsletter and served as the public relations person for the program where she worked, so I know those journalism skills she'd learned at Franklin and in college were coming in handy.

"No, I never saw Cheron again after Ohio, and I missed out on meeting your dad and you and Phillip. I had a massive heart attack and died when you were only months old. But, guess what? I've kept my eye on you all these years and tried to maintain the spirit love link between Heaven and your family down on Earth. I think your mom felt my love and influence, even if she never got around to telling you about Helen and me."

"She told me about your cat, Houdini, who opened your front door!" I laughed at the thought of that tricky cat. We hugged one another and I told Uncle Bob how Steve had been asking me lots of questions about my life on Earth. "Hey, when I tell my life story to Steve, why don't you come, too? You can help me with the remembering."

"It's a deal, Scotty. I think you're getting to be a good storyteller, just like your Uncle Alex and GG. It would be fun to hear what you remember about the days in New Mexico and Oregon. For now, we'd better skedaddle down and see what's on the menu for dinner. I'm hungry as a bear."

22 The Compassionate Friends

One day in early November Mom got a call from a local nurse who was a doctor's wife. Jackie had heard about my dying in July and she knew Mom was studying to be a counselor. She was especially concerned about the families of children who died. Her husband was a children's doctor and losing a patient was always hard on him. This nurse lady was also in a counselor training program and she was hoping to start a group for families to help them get over their grief. It was called The Compassionate Friends. There were support groups springing up all over the United States and in England. Mom and Jackie got together for lunch and then decided to see if other parents wanted to be part of such a group. They put an article in the newspaper and sent a notice to all the kids' doctors in town.

Even before the scheduled meeting at Jackie's house, many parents called Mom or Jackie to say they'd want to be part of the group. Each caller had a unique story to tell, but every one was struggling in similar ways and hoping the chance to share would bring some relief and some answers to take away the pain. Some of the phone calls were very long because Mom was a good listener and the parent who was calling needed someone to talk to. Mom told Dad it worked best if she put on her "clinical counselor hat" to keep some distance so she didn't end up crying every time she hung up the phone. Nevertheless, it was impossible for her not to share from her heart and tell about losing me and our family's ongoing grief work. She knew this was good experience and information for the research she planned in writing her college paper.

One caller was a young nurse whose healthy baby had died suddenly in his crib. She said, "Even though I work in the hospital with other people's sick children, my baby boy died one night right in our own house." She felt guilty for not being able to prevent it, but the doctor told her the baby died of a mysterious illness called SIDS, Sudden Infant Death Syndrome, and she couldn't have known it might happen. "I dream of him every night," she said, "and I just can't make myself go back to work on the pediatrics ward. Sometimes I have an awful fear of these other children dying in my care, and sometimes I just get mad because other parents' kids get well and thrive, but mine died."

An older dad called. His wife was right next to him while he talked on the phone. "We lost our college-age daughter. She was raped, tortured and murdered by a serial killer in California. All the publicity was driving us crazy so we had to move far away." He went on to describe how beautiful and smart the girl was. They figured they'd never be able to make sense about what had happened, but they had learned a lot about grieving and wanted to share their story and get ideas from other parents.

"My little Ann lived only a few minutes," related another mother. "I never had a chance to get to know her. The doctor suspected she had some sort of deformity, so we tried to prepare ourselves. But she was born without a brain and didn't have a chance to survive. The nurses were great; they dressed her in the frilly newborn dress we had brought to the hospital, and they found a bonnet that covered the missing part of her head. We got to hold her for a little while before she went to the mortuary. We're really scared to think about having another baby, even though the doctor says it should be okay. I hope there'll be other parents in the group who can understand and help us."

My dad, Bill, came home from the Emergency room one night with a very heavy heart. "I was patching up the many broken bones of a beautiful teenage girl. She and her boyfriend were taking her little brother, who was a high school football hero, downtown to a movie. A couple of other cars were racing on Fairgrounds Road and one of them slammed into the car at high speed. The brother died instantly, my patient will have a long recuperation if she's ever to walk again, and the boyfriend who was driving is bereft with guilt as he deals with his own physical injuries. And the parents, Cheron...they are a salt-of-the-earth family that doesn't deserve such sorrow. Well," he mused with sadness, "I guess none of us deserves to lose our kids, and the children certainly don't deserve to die. Damn, it's just so infuriating, isn't it? I think they're going to need your Compassionate Friends group."

Jackie had fielded even more phone calls, each with a heartbreaking story of child loss. She and Mom shared some of this information by phone and talked about how they might prepare to run a group that would be helpful so that parents would want to come back after the first meeting. Mom had facilitated support groups for patients with rheumatoid arthritis in Albuquerque, and for minority youth who were trying to change their lives from drug addiction to gainful employment. Her job as a graduate assistant at Oregon State was to help Masters-level students explore their own values and attributes as they prepared to become counselors. She ran a group for that. This situation of children dying and families grieving was new to her, except for what she'd learned from reading books like *Death Be Not Proud*, *A Death in the Family*, William Allen White's autobiography, or the play *All My Sons* from high school drama days.

"I have just started gathering books and articles to use in my doctoral research," she told Jackie. "Frankly, I haven't been in an emotional place where I wanted to read the clinical stuff, but rather have looked for knowledge and inspiration from parents who have 'been there.' That's harder to find. Elisabeth Kubler-Ross' work on death and dying is in the popular literature right now, including her reports of the hospice movement, and near-death experiences where people claim they perceive the afterlife. I am developing a good familiarity with these so I'll bring that knowledge to the group."

"The brochure I got from The Compassionate Friends lists a couple of recently published books I can acquire," said Jackie. "Have you heard of *The Bereaved Parent* or *Death Comes Home?*"

"I'd like to read both after you're through," said Mom. "Let's be ready with some of this information to generate discussion if the group goes silent. My guess, however, is that parents will be anxious to talk in a supportive, protective environment of understanding peers, and we'll have more trouble keeping just one or two from dominating the conversation, or keeping the tone open and accepting as well as reasonably hopeful and positive."

Mom and Jackie hurried to gather the group before Thanksgiving knowing that the upcoming family holidays were going to be tough. Plowing through books was very time-consuming, but Mom remembered to check her "thought file." That was the recipe-card box of quotes and ideas she had started at the suggestion of Uncle Bob, who was Mr. Wettleson to her back in high school. He had told his students this was a good technique for journalists and writers to store ideas they might refer to later when they were writing an article or preparing a speech. Since Mom had been building her file for fifteen years, it was pretty full. She pulled a few quotes that might come in handy for the group:

> The disappointments in life are meant to make us better, not bitter.

> Faith is the bird that feels the light and sings when the dawn is still dark. *(Rabindranth Tagore)*

> The past cannot be changed, but the future is still in your power.

> Positive anything is better than negative nothing.

> Worry is like sand in an oyster: A little makes a pearl, too much will kill the animal.

> The brook would lose its song if we removed all the rocks.

> Acting and Giving are not necessarily more useful than Resting and Receiving. *(Wayne Miller)*

Hope is like the sun which, as we journey toward it, casts the shadow of our burdens behind us. *(Samuel Smiles)*

If you are not as close to your God as you used to be, there is absolutely no question as to who has moved.

I am determined to be cheerful and happy in whatever situation I might be. For I have learned from experience that the greater part of our happiness or misery depends on our disposition and not on our circumstances. *(Martha Washington)*

Mom thought, "Some of these seem pretty trite and I don't know who originally said most of them, but every one has given me a lift or a shove at some juncture along the way. Can't hurt to keep them in mind to share if the need and occasion arises in the group."

Twenty-seven mothers and fathers showed up at Jackie's house for the first meeting. They were told not to bring kids. Jackie gave an introduction explaining how The Compassionate Friends organization was working for so many bereaved parents. This, she said, was a beginning framework, but there was no set way in which this group had to develop. It all depended on what the members wanted and needed. Coffee, tea and cookies were provided and the houseful of people squeezed closely together, sitting on the floor and every available seat Jackie could gather from all over the house and patio.

It turned out there was no need to have worried about silence and lack of sharing. These folks were anxious to share their stories and connect with others whose hearts had been broken because their children had died. Seems this was an outlet they'd been desperate for. Many said they no longer felt comfortable talking about their grief with friends and relatives who had their own lives to lead and had moved on after the death event. Jackie had been wise to place boxes of tissue around the room because the tears flowed freely. No one who spoke felt it necessary to hold back or escape because it was unbearable; everyone knew that this group really did know how they were feeling. Each story was received with affirming nods, hugs, or pats on the back. The three hours passed very quickly. The group unanimously agreed to meet again in early December.

When Mom and Jackie debriefed and began planning the next session, they decided the one thing they needed to guard against was "oneupsmanship." That is, one parent speaking as if his or her situation was far worse than anyone else's. "I have had my own pity parties these past few months, when I couldn't imagine anyone suffering more intensely than I," said Mom. "But, with the reading I've done and the stories I have heard, I'm convinced that child loss and grief are unique and devastating experiences for each parent. No one can judge one from the other. I used to think I was robbed of so many years that would have been enjoyed by parents who didn't lose their child until he or she was a teenager or older. And I figured the violence and suddenness of Scotty's death was far worse than losing a sick or injured child over a period of weeks, months or years. They have a term for this -- 'anticipatory grief.' Then I started thinking about parents of children who had been murdered or committed suicide. I'm now convinced it does no good to make such comparisons and think of other bereaved parents as more lucky than I. We are all extremely unlucky on an equal basis. We need to get that across in the group. We are coming together to help one another, not to align ourselves along a scale of who's been dealt the worst blow."

Jackie nodded. "Amen to that. Let's try to get people talking more about what has been useful in their healing. Many mentioned their faith and church connections. Some talked about books they'd found or special friendships. All in all, I'm excited by what transpired. We'd better find a bigger venue for the December meeting!"

23 Thanksgiving, Green Peas and Football

Long before Thanksgiving the stores were full of Christmas decorations. I remember how Mom bargain-shopped for gifts all year long and hid them away until December. Last year Phillip and I found a box of wrapped presents in the water heater closet. We wanted to open the ones with our names on them but Mom used lots of tape and tied ribbons very tight. I tore the paper, ripping off Rudolph's head, before I decided I didn't want to get in big trouble with Mom. Besides, I really like surprises and was afraid I'd be too disappointed on Christmas morning if I knew what I was getting from my parents even before Santa had a chance to leave stuff under the tree. Phillip made a real mess of his gift so I helped him use a whole roll of Scotch tape to put it back together. I guess Mom didn't notice because she never said anything about it.

This year Mom felt a heartache every time she considered the holidays without me so she avoided shopping altogether. She needed to send the box of Douglas fir cones to New Hampshire in time for her friend to use them in wreath-making. That was all the Christmas activity she was willing to take on in November. She had asked Elizabeth to make a cone-art decoration for my grave at the cemetery. By December first it came in the mail – an upright spaceship that looked like it was ready to blast off. It was a lot better than all the flower wreaths or potted plants on other graves, and tough enough to last until Valentine's Day.

Dad had four season tickets to all the Seahawk home football games in Seattle. I had always liked the weekend trips in the fall because I got to see some of my cousins. Dad gave Phillip and me a choice of going to the game or staying that Sunday at Uncle Alex's or Auntie Alice's house. Whoever agreed to babysit us got to decide how to use our tickets for the game. Phillip loved the noise and the crowds at the Kingdome so he usually went to see the Seahawks, but I looked forward to playing with Darren Kelly or Andre and checking out all their toys. The Seattle motels we stayed in were cheap because Mom said all we needed was a clean bed and a warm shower. My favorite one was on Aurora Avenue. We usually tried to get the upstairs room that was built out over the driveway in front of the office. It had a cozy closet with a window and a door, and that's what I called my own bedroom. I slept on the closet floor in my sleeping bag so Phillip had a bed all to himself.

In the months after I died, my family gave most of the football tickets away because they didn't have the energy to make the trip. By November, though, staying busy and getting out of Salem seemed to help the lonely days go by a little faster. My parents got together with Auntie Alice and her husband for Sunday brunch before the game. The four of them decided the two families should go skiing together in Idaho during the week of Christmas. That way there would be more family together and not the loneliness of the Mayhalls at home, missing me. Mom had already decided not to put up a decorated tree in the living room nor hang the Christmas stockings she'd made, one for each of us, with our names on them. We usually had five or six to hang because we made them for the pets, too. The one for our former dog, Sonya, was still packed with the Christmas stuff, but Mom hadn't remembered to make a new one for Heidi-pie. That would have to wait until next year. Decorating the whole house so soon after my death would make everyone too sad. Instead, they'd simply put lights on the Norfolk pine planted next to our driveway in memory of me and, of course, the front door would have the cone wreath from New Hampshire.

Several couples from our church who had young children, but who lived too far from the grandparents to travel over the Thanksgiving weekend, threw a big turkey potluck dinner for the Thursday feast. They, too, knew the day would be very sad if my little family had only three settings at the table where there should have been four. Five families gathered in the church fellowship hall. The moms worked in the kitchen and set the tables with candles and autumn leaves while the dads talked about football and Phillip had a blast playing with the other boys and girls. The prayers and grace included asking God to help my family get healed and happy again. They all sang some hymns and Mom got all teary when they sang the words from "Now Thank We All Our God:"

> ...God, through all our life be near us, with blessed peace to cheer us...
> Keep us in God's grace, Guide us when perplexed...
> Free us from all ills in this world and the next.

The day after Thanksgiving, when our family usually ate hot turkey sandwiches and the rest of the pumpkin pie, Dad had his appointment for the operation which could help him make babies again. I didn't want to watch the surgery while it was going on in the operating room, but Uncle Alex told me after it was over that it was no big deal. I giggled because he said Dad had a sore groin and he was told to lie around and watch football games with a bag of frozen peas on his privates! When GG served peas mixed with carrots for our Thanksgiving leftovers dinner in Heaven, I couldn't help thinking of Dad lying there with his frozen peas, watching his Longhorns play the Texas Aggies.

All the adoption forms and the down payment to get another child through the Holt Agency were due in Eugene by early December. The application was encouraging and hopeful, so Mom seemed to feel a bit happier and allowed herself to do some Christmas shopping and planning after that. She bought a child-angel statue for Granny to set up on her bookcase as a reminder of me. Granny had fifteen grandchildren and some were already teenagers, but I was the littlest. The bigger ones didn't seem very angelic most days, but Granny still had no problem imagining me as an angel. I know she believed I was keeping an eye on her. She even seemed to sense that Uncle Alex and I were together in Heaven.

Mom got a call from another college girlfriend, Dorothy, who lived in San Francisco. Dorothy was writing notes on Christmas cards when she decided she needed to talk to Mom in person, not just on paper. Dorothy's father had been the chemistry professor at Pacific University until he had a heart attack and died suddenly in 1975. Dorothy's whole family had become friends to Mom during the college years. "Thinking of you and your family during this lonely time without Scotty has me reminiscing about the year after my father died. I especially recall the holidays," Dorothy explained, "because those were the hardest. Nothing and no one could fill the void; we just had to develop new ways of celebrating that weren't dependent on his physical presence. But I want you to know that it gets easier after you've been through a complete year's cycle of all the birthdays, holidays, family reunions, and such. I know you've had a rough year just missing Alex, but Scotty's death is bound to be even more difficult because you depended on him being there every day, every night. Hang in there and believe what I'm telling you. Christmas is painful this year, but it'll be much better in 1978. I love you guys."

The night Phillip asked Mom to read him *The Littlest Angel* was very tough for her. Fortunately, Phillip knew it by heart and could read it perfectly well all by himself. He ended up reading it out loud for both of them. Mom cried most of the way through, looking at the familiar pictures of the little-boy angel who was just my age when he died. He had a box of earthly treasures, much like the blue memory box Granddaddy had made for my toys and equipment. "I love the happy ending," said Phillip, "where the little boy gets to meet the Christ Child. Just think, Mom, Scotty has probably been talking with Jesus up there in Heaven. And flying, just like he always wanted! Don't cry. I think Scotty and the other angels are singing and having a good time."

Mom always wrote a cheery holiday letter to tell everyone about the highlights of our year. She and Dad had sent out the letter with a picture of the family every Christmas since they got married, even when the family was just the two of them, or when their first "child" was actually a dog, Sonya. This year it was hard to be cheery, so

Mom decided to write a short greeting and introduction, then include a copy of what she'd written in August about me dying before I had time to grow up and become an astronaut. Instead of having someone take a family photo, which Dad always hated posing for, Mom chose a snapshot of Phillip in his yellow sweatsuit in front of the fireplace with Heidi. It took me by surprise to see that Heidi's St. Bernard head was now almost twice as big as Phillip's head! Heidi's big brown eyes looked very sad, but she was beautiful and I missed her. Phillip looked beautiful in the picture, too, and I missed him almost as much as Heidi.

Some of the people on the Christmas letter list hadn't heard about the accident yet. They called or wrote nice notes, and a few wanted to donate money to the playground at Little Beavers. Three people sent tree ornaments that were angels. Two were cherubs and one was Charlie Brown's Snoopy dog wearing a Santa Claus hat and angel wings. Mom had already decided not to put up a tree, especially since they were leaving the day before Christmas on the ski trip to Sun Valley with Auntie Alice's family. But the angel ornaments gave her an idea about making our Christmas trees a memorial. She bought two more ornaments at the Hallmark store. One was a fuzzy, brown teddy-bear angel cuddling on a cloud, and the other was a soft gray mouse angel singing Christmas carols and wearing a halo. She planned to have enough angel ornaments by the next Christmas to hang one on every branch and call it the "Scotty Memorial Tree."

Most of the Christmas carols had words about joy and angels. Joy was my mother's middle name and she had always liked it, but this year she wasn't feeling very full of joy. Yet, it was hard not to sing along, and she could imagine Scotty singing with a choir of angels, just as Phillip had envisioned it.

I asked GG if we were going to have a Christmas tree and all that stuff in Heaven. "Well," she said, "some of the children in our house are not Christians and they usually are from families where other winter holidays are celebrated instead of Christmas. Uncle

Alex and I have decided to honor all of the religious celebrations by encouraging and helping each child to develop a strong spirit link with their friends and families back on Earth. That way they can continue to enjoy the parts of the holidays that made them feel happy, and their loved ones will feel their spirit presence even stronger."

After that, when "Frosty the Snowman" or "Rudolph the Red-nosed Reindeer" came on the radio or television, or started playing in the supermaket, I closed my eyes real tight and sang along as loud as I could: "…with a corncob pipe and a button nose and two eyes made out of coal…", or "…then one foggy Christmas Eve, Santa came to say, 'Rudolph with your nose so bright, won't you guide my sleigh tonight?'…" My spirit-voice must have gotten through to Earth because my Mom or Phillip usually cracked a smile and started singing along with me and the guys on the record.

24   *Little Beavers Christmas*

The owners and staff at Little Beavers called to invite Mom, Dad and Phillip to attend the preschool Christmas program on December 12. It was "dedicated to the memory of Scotty Mayhall" and my picture was on the programs they handed out. They also quoted the verse Dad composed for my gravestone: "Scotty wanted to be an astronaut. Now he flies with angels. We will always love him."

I asked Uncle Alex, Steve and the other kids at my heavenly home to watch the program with me. Earlier that week we had been invited by Esther to watch her Earth family's celebration of Hanukkah and we learned about dreidels and lighting the menorah candles. Now it was my turn to show them how my Christian preschool honored the Baby Jesus' birth.

The classes with the littlest kids, Tigers and Elephants, put on costumes for a pageant showing how things looked in the stable where the Christ Child was born. Katy and Kelly got to be Mary and Joseph. Since there weren't any tigers and elephants in Bethlehem, the other toddlers dressed like goats, cows, sheep, horses and a dove. They sang "Away in a Manger" and "Jesus Our Brother." They forgot some of the words and sang out of tune, but all the parents clapped and laughed as if it sounded perfect. The kindergarten class put on a play, *The Shoemaker and the Elves*, and sang "Rudolph" and "Santa Claus is Coming to Town." Steve and I knew most of the words so we could sing along from our perch in Heaven.

The middle part of the program was all about me and featured my best friends at Little Beavers. My four-year-old class was called The Star Warriors. To begin, Al East, the man who owned the school, read a eulogy he'd written. It was both funny and sad, so pretty much all the other parents joined Mom and Dad as they cried and laughed their way through the stories remembering me. Then The Star Warriors lined up to sing my very favorite song of all time, "Miss Mary Mac." Uncle Alex scooted over and took me into his lap with a broad grin on his face. "Oh Scotty," he chuckled, "this is the song everyone loved to hear you sing. Do you remember how you substituted "w's" for all the "r's", and we all learned to sing it that way, too? Let's you and I sing along now."

> Miss May-we Mac, Mac, Mac
> All dwessed in black, black, black
> With silvew buttons, buttons, buttons
> All down huw back, back, back.
>
> She asked huw mothew, mothew, mothew
> Fow fifteen cents, cents, cents
> To see the elephants, elephants, elephants
> Jump the fence, fence, fence.
>
> They jumped so high, high, high
> They weached the sky, sky, sky

And they nevuw came back, back, back
Til the fowth of July, ly, ly.

I had forgotten how I talked and sang a little bit funny when I was alive. Now all my buddies in Heaven giggled as Unk and I sang. I was thinking my friends and family at Little Beavers must have heard the chorus from Heaven, too. It made me feel very warm and happy at the same time I was feeling a little lonely. I was glad Unk was there to hold me in his lap. When Santa Claus showed up at the end of the program, GG called us into her kitchen for gingerbread cookies and milk while the kids on Earth were getting oranges and candy canes.

A few days later Jackie and Mom held the second meeting for The Compassionate Friends group. The invitations and newspaper announcement suggested that bereaved parents bring snapshots and a happy story about the child who died. They gathered in the fellowship hall of the Congregational Church where they could have soothing background music, candlelight, and serve Christmas cookies and red punch. Some of the parents couldn't wait for the meeting to start before showing their pictures and sharing their child's story. When they finally gathered in the circled chairs, the mood became very solemn and there wasn't much talking. Many of them held hands with the person next to them, even if they never met that person before.

Later, when Mom arrived home and Dad asked her how it had gone, she said, "I'm sure everyone wanted to see the pictures of the babies, toddlers, school kids, teenagers and even some adults, but only a few chose to do this in the quiet of the circle. I think most of us knew we couldn't get through telling a happy story without crying, so we just sat there listening to the wonderful music. They seemed to appreciate the comfort of fleeing the hustle and bustle of Christmas on the outside and finding fellowship with others who could fathom the depths of their loneliness and grief. One couple tearfully told Jackie how grateful they were for compassion and sanctuary. They're going to host the January meeting at their real estate offices."

25   A Blessed Event

On December 20, Mom began packing for the ski trip to Sun Valley. Auntie Alice, Uncle Maynard and their three boys would be driving from Seattle to meet them there on the twenty-fourth. Phillip would love skiing and playing in the snow with David, Daniel and Darren Kelly, and the four parents knew they'd made an unspoken pact to support each other through this first Christmas after I died. It would be better far away from our house and in a winter wonderland where they could keep active on the slopes all day. Auntie Alice and Mom would enjoy cooking together in the condo for the meals they wouldn't eat in restaurants. The moms and kids loved to play Scrabble and Junior Scrabble.

Everything was almost set for the departure from Salem as soon as Dad got off work on December 23. Then, the phone rang. Dad said from his office, "Cheron, I just learned that a baby girl has been born this morning at the maternity hospital and she's available for us to adopt if we want her. What do you think?"

"Right now?!" Mom gasped. "We're supposed to leave town in just a few hours. Oh, but a baby girl…my heart is about to beat through my chest, Bill! I think I want to get a baby for Christmas. What do you think?"

"Well, you'll have to call Seattle and Sun Valley right now to cancel our travel plans. I'm told we weren't on the top of the list, but the number-one family says they want to hold out for a boy, and the second family has already gone to Mexico for the holidays. The lawyer and the hospital want to release the newborn in two days, so we have to decide right now."

"Okay. Yes, yes. Yes! What else do you know about the baby girl?"

"Not much, actually. I know the doctor who delivered her and he wouldn't be moving her out of the hospital nursery so quickly if she weren't very healthy. The phone call I got was from the baby's attorney. It's a closed adoption so we can't know the parents. He tells me the birth mother is only fourteen and there's no information about the father. The baby weighs something like eight pounds and has thick, black hair. She is Caucasian."

"Oh, Bill. I can't believe this. What a miracle – an answer to prayer. I haven't been praying for a baby so much as just praying for a way to survive this Christmas season without Scotty. Okay, what am I supposed to do next? I don't have any baby clothes or blankets. The crib is dismantled in the attic. We'll need to buy diapers, baby bottles and formula…"

"Slow down, honey. The attorney said to call his office for instructions. If you're sure about this, call 555-379-4302. His secretary will tell you exactly what's up. Call me back. I have to see patients until 2:30 and then make rounds at the hospital. Call my secretary and she'll track me down. I love you." He hung up and she stood there trembling.

Mom was so nervous she had trouble dialing the phone and talking. "Hello. My name is Cheron. I'm Dr. Mayhall's wife. He told me to call you about the baby girl. We want very much to adopt her. Umm, do we need to fill out forms or anything like that? Umm…sorry, I'm so excited I don't know what to do or say."

"That's okay," said the lady on the phone. " I've been hoping you'd call. We'll get all the duckies in a row so you'll have that wee one in your arms on Christmas day. All you need to do, for starters, is take some newborn pajamas and a warm blanket to Dr. James' office on Main Street. They'll dress the child in the clothes you choose and release her from the hospital to my boss. You mustn't go to the hospital or talk to anyone about what's going on. If you can do this, I'll call you tomorrow morning to set up a time on the twenty-fifth when you can come to our offices and take the baby home."

"Okay. Sure, that's easy," Mom said. "I have to make a couple of phone calls to clear our schedule for the next few days, but

I can get these things to Dr. James by two o'clock. I'll wait here for your call tomorrow, or you can reach my husband through his answering service. Thank you so much." The tears of joy began to flow. "Thank you so much."

Composing herself, she called Auntie Alice to explain the change of plans. "Well," said her sister, "that's amazing. A brand new baby. Today? I always wanted a girl. Let me call Idaho to cancel our reservations. We have all next week off. Can we visit you in Salem to meet the baby? Oh, this is so amazing! Just do what you need to do there and call me when you know more. I won't tell Mom or the rest of the Seattle family until it's a done deal, okay?"

"Perfect. Thanks, Alice. I"ll get back to you. Maybe even this evening."

After reporting her progress to Dad and dropping Phillip next door at Gramma Edna's, Mom went to the baby store in the mall. She chose a red, stretch pajama suit with a fur-trimmed Santa hat. "I gave away all our baby things as Scotty outgrew them," she remembered. "I didn't have baby girl things anyhow. But we had chosen a girl name: Laura Belinda Joy Mayhall. Bill thought it was quirky to give a child the initials of the famous President from Texas, LBJ. But it has a good lilt to it. I have always loved the name Laura, especially as it belongs to my college friend who has the voice of an angel and is a gifted pianist. Belinda: 'pretty' or 'beautiful' in Spanish, and a name I heard frequently when I lived in Latin America. And Joy, after me, just as we gave Bill's names to both Phillip and Scotty. Anyhow, what could be more perfect than to name the Christmas baby 'Joy'?"

At Dr. James' office she remembered her instructions not to discuss this baby business with anyone. The receptionist was asking a lot of questions she couldn't answer, unaccustomed to having walk-ins off the street asking for an immediate appointment. Seeing Mom's discomfort and wanting to be discrete, she asked Mom to be seated in the waiting room and the doctor would see her shortly.

Then a nurse came and escorted Mom to an exam room, handing her a hospital gown and a cup for a urine sample. "I don't think I need an exam," Mom stammered. "I'd just like to talk briefly with Dr. James."

"Well," replied the nurse, "it's customary to do a pelvic exam and get a urine sample on the first office visit. Please use the bathroom across the hall and push this button when you're gowned and ready."

"Okay," Mom nodded as the nurse left the room. "Lord, they must be thinking, 'here's a 35-year-old doctor's wife whose had an affair, got herself knocked up and is too immature to even talk about it!'" She was mortified, but she dutifully went to the bathroom and got the sample. She decided not to undress before pushing the button.

A few minutes later, Dr. James and his nurse came in. He was very kind and introduced himself before asking what he could do for her. Mom still hesitated to talk about the baby in front of the nurse, but felt she had no choice.

"Dr. James," she began, "My husband and I were told by an attorney that I should come talk with you about adopting a new baby girl, but that I shouldn't mention it to anyone else. I'm feeling very peculiar about all this, but I don't think I need a pelvic exam, right?" Then she held out the cup of urine and the bag containing the baby pajamas and blanket.

The doctor chuckled, set the urine and the bag aside, and took her hands. "Oh, yes, Cheron Mayhall. It's nice to meet you. Sorry about all the confusion. You are right – no pelvic necessary. I'll just see that these clothing items get to the hospital and the baby's attorney will instruct you further. Do you have any questions I might answer now?"

Still rosy-cheeked with embarrassment, Mom said, "It's all happening so fast. Of course, we are thrilled about the baby, but we are totally ignorant about the process and don't want to make any blunders. I'll have to go shopping for some more baby things, won't

I? Oh, we can't wait to see the child, hopefully by Christmas."

"Surely," said the kindly doctor. "You just try to relax and everything will be fine. The hospital will send a cardboard cradle and a layette so you'll have a starter supply of formula, diapers and the like. You don't need to worry about shopping until after Christmas. This will be the merry Christmas you and Bill deserve after the sorrow you've endured. I'm very happy for you."

He walked her to the door and she escaped without having to catch the eye of the curious nurse and receptionist. Once in the car she tried deep breathing and a little meditation to get her bearings. When she picked up Phillip at Gramma Edna's house, she told him that the ski trip had been cancelled but that they were going to get a very special Christmas delivery and that Auntie Alice's family would be coming to visit during the holidays.

Up in Heaven I hadn't actually been paying close attention to Earth happenings since watching the Christmas program at Little Beavers. Steve and I had been making a Lego village on the floor of our bedroom. We couldn't decide whether it was a town in the Old West or a settlement on Mars, so we used it for both, one day inhabited by cowboy and Indian action figures and the next day by space creatures and astronauts. We didn't really know what creatures were in outer space, but we had our dinosaur toys that worked just fine. Our moms didn't like any stories or TV shows that had killing and dying, so our creatures didn't eat people and our western figures didn't fight each another. In Heaven they lived in peace and helped one another.

Anyhow, it finally dawned on me that something really important was going on down there. When I tuned in and heard my Mom telling Auntie Alice about Dad's phone call and her trip to the doctor's office, I couldn't believe my ears. I told Steve, "I think God has answered our prayers. My Mom's talking about getting a baby girl!" We ran downstairs to find Uncle Alex and GG so they could confirm what I suspected. They surveyed the situation and said they got the same impression. "Yes," said GG, "it appears that Bill and Cheron are going to adopt a little baby, and soon."

Steve yelled, "Yippee!" He'd been saying that word a lot when our action figures got on bucking broncos at the rodeo in our Lego town. "Yippee! God has been listening to our prayers every night. We have to thank Him right now." We grabbed Unk and GG by their hands and pulled them down on their knees right there in the living room. With heads bowed, we each took a turn praising God for His goodness in getting this Christmas baby. Steve reminded God, "Don't forget that my Earth family also needs a baby boy, as soon as you can get around to it. "

When Mom phoned Auntie Alice with the latest update, Uncle Maynard answered the phone. He expressed reservations about the adoption. "I don't think you should jump into this so quickly. What if the baby has some serious health issues? She might be retarded, or her parents might cause you some problems. Think about it: you don't need any more grief right now. You haven't even seen her yet and you're talking as if she's yours. Please, Cheron, think this through."

Auntie Alice wrested the phone from her husband and tried to smooth over his negativity. "You know 'Maynard the pessimist' generally sees the worst case scenario when things like this sneak up out of his control. I believe this baby is a special gift from God to help rebuild your family. It couldn't come at a better time. Don't worry, we'll come down on Tuesday and I expect Maynard will fall in love with your Laura. He's a sucker for babies. She'll wrap him around her little finger in sixty seconds flat."

"Don't worry about it, Alice," said Mom. "In some of my reading I've seen warnings about trying to find a 'replacement child.' That's not healthy. But I think we are mature enough to know Scotty is irreplaceable. A new child will help to fill the void. I'm glad it's a girl, not a boy."

26 The Joy of Christmas

Dad had time on the twenty-fourth to bring the crib, cradle and toy box down from the attic. All three had been hand-crafted by Granddaddy for his own little boys, my dad and his older brother. Phillip watched with curiosity and asked a lot of questions. "Are you going to give away Scotty's crib? Do you remember how I rocked Scotty in that cradle when he was tiny and I was two? Hey, can I have that toy box in my room? I bet I'm going to need some more space for my toys after Santa comes tonight."

Dad smiled and decided it was time to let Phillip in on the secret that was unfolding. "How about you help me put the crib together and we'll set it up in Scotty's old room next door to yours? That special delivery Mom told you about is going to be a real live baby sister for you. We are going to adopt her tomorrow, and you will get your wish to be a big brother again."

The wheels were turning in Phillip's head. "You mean, the baby won't have to be in Mom's tummy? Is this going to be one of those stork deliveries?"

"No," explained Dad, "adoption means that the baby comes out of the tummy of another woman, but that our home and family have been chosen to help her grow up. She'll be our daughter and your sister forever. The other mom and dad aren't ready for all the responsibilities of raising a child. We are, aren't we, Phillip? Can you be ready by tomorrow to welcome a new baby into the Mayhall family?"

"Sure I will," Paul said, his face beaming. "Two of the kids at school are adopted. Their parents got them from China and Mexico. Is our baby coming from China or Mexico?"

"No, she's coming straight from the hospital here in town. You can go with Mom and me tomorrow afternoon when we pick her up. So, let's get busy and have this crib ready for her. If you have a soft toy you'd like to share with her, we'll put it in the crib to comfort the baby." With that, Phillip went to his room and gathered up every single stuffed animal he could find, except his Barnaby Bear. He could never part with Barnaby, even for a new baby sister.

On Christmas Eve the family went to the early candlelight service at the church. Pastor Ed and many friends greeted them with knowing hugs, understanding how difficult it must be getting through Christmas with me gone and in Heaven. Ordinarily Mom would have read *The Littlest Angel* at the early service but it wasn't even part of the program this year. Mom decided to focus on the hope and joy at the heart of the Christmas story and the doll baby displayed in the manger cradle up near the altar. "By this time tomorrow we'll have our Baby Laura," she thought. When everyone was sipping wassail and passing around the seasons greetings after the service, Mom couldn't contain her secret. She hugged her good friend, Elaine, and whispered in her ear, " Now don't let on about this secret I'm about to tell you…we are going to adopt a baby girl tomorrow!" Elaine's eyes teared up and she beamed with delight, but she didn't scream or do anything that would make other people suspicious.

After Phillip was in bed on Christmas Eve, Dad ate Santa's cookies while Mom put some wrapped presents in front of the fireplace. I guessed they'd written to Santa in the North Pole so he knew they'd be going to Idaho. With the sudden change of plans, my parents just pretended Santa was coming to our house, for Phillip's sake. They went to bed just after midnight, but excitement about the baby kept them from sleeping much.

Dad had purchased a toy train set for Phillip. He thought he'd be setting it up at the condo in Sun Valley for all four boys to play with. It was Phillip's favorite gift when he tore into his packages early on Christmas morning. Now the two of them were aligning the tracks and creating the village around the station in the middle of the family room floor. Heidi-pie wagged her tail and became very curious when they got the thing going round and round in circles. Phillip scolded her when she knocked the engine over with her big paws. She retreated and patiently waited in the hall for a time when she might be the center of attention. Mom was puttering and daydreaming in my old bedroom that had been changed into a guest room, and now into a nursery. She was thinking of how she'd furnish and decorate the space with a color scheme of winter white and red, and a butterfly theme.

After eating a light lunch, the three Mayhalls visited my grave at the cemetery. The pine cone spaceship from New Hampshire and a holly wreath from Uncle Alex's wife were already laid. Now they added four red roses, one for each year I'd lived with them on Earth, and one for each of our family members. Mom whispered to Dad, "I'm not sure if the fourth honors Scotty or Laura at this point. Maybe I should have brought five roses." Phillip arranged the blooms in an arc on the grave stone. Wiping away tears, they departed.

At 3:30 p.m. they headed for the lawyer's office to pick up the baby girl. They rode the elevator to the fourth floor, squeezing each other's hands in nervous excitement. When the elevator door opened, the first thing they saw was a tall man holding a baby tucked into a large red Christmas stocking. The white fur trim on her hat contrasted boldly with the shock of dark hair. The lawyer settled Baby Laura gently into my mom's arms. Breathless and feeling weak in the knees, she sat down quickly in the nearest chair.

"She's a gorgeous little angel," Mom murmured, and all people present nodded their heads in agreement. Phillip reached out to run his fingers through the baby's hair. "Mom, you only got bald babies before, right?" he exclaimed. Dad knelt down and encircled his family with his arms as they all gazed in wonderment at the newest Mayhall.

"The nurses in the newborn nursery had a hard time letting this one go," said Laura's lawyer. "Those who work the holiday shifts make a big deal of these Christmas babies and send them home in big red stockings. They've also sent her cardboard cradle and diapers and formula to get you started." He paused. "Now, Bill, you'll need to put me in touch with your own lawyer so we can take care of all the legal business. The state requires their agency to make a home visit, so a social worker will be calling you next week to set a time for that. If you don't have any further questions, you are welcome to take your new daughter home now. What do you think about that, Phillip?"

"I'm going to be a good big brother," he boasted. "Can I hold her? Does she cry? I want to see her eyes and hear her voice."

They all squeezed into the front seat of the car with Phillip in the middle so he could gaze at the baby and hold onto her feet in the toe of the giant felt stocking. "We're going to name her Laura Belinda Joy," Mom told Phillip. "She's our 'Laura Bundle-a-Joy'," he mused. Mom looked across at Dad who was grinning from ear to ear. On the car radio Debbie Boone was singing "You Light Up My Life." Mom decided that had to be the baby's theme song. She sang the lyrics with Debbie:

> You light up my life, you give me hope to carry on.
> You light up my days, and fill my nights with song.
> It can't be wrong, when it feels so right.
> 'Cause you, you light up my life.

Because Dad had mentioned to one of his doctor friends about the change of plans for Idaho, my family was invited for a late Christmas supper at the doctor's home in south Salem. Imagine how surprised the hostess was when she opened the door to see a baby bundle in Mom's arms. Laura woke up and cooed to the pleasure of all during the supper visit. The evening was so warm and joyous, my parents knew they'd turned a page on their sadness and things were going to be happier from this day forward.

At home, Phillip needed a quick refresher course on how to hold a baby bottle. They clustered around the precious bundle on the couch and started making calls to spread the happy news. Gramma Edna and Grampa Larry came right over from next door. Godmother Sue let out such a squeal of delight you could have heard it all the way from New York even if she wasn't on the phone.

Auntie Alice cried as Mom described the baby. "I didn't get a girl of my own, but I'm going to be the best auntie in the world for Laura. I will call the rest of our family here in Seattle. I think Mom will probably want to drive to Salem with us on Tuesday to see her newest grandchild. We'll bring our sleeping bags and sleep on your floor."

When the neighbors departed, the house quieted down and Mom changed Laura's wet diaper. She sat rocking the baby beside the fireplace and humming "You Light Up My Life." It made me think of Mary with her baby, Jesus, and I noticed our whole house and yard seemed to have a halo glow around it. I felt peace and happiness in my heart, the most I'd felt since arriving in Heaven. And I knew that Christmas Joy had come to my earthly home at last.

27 *Bundle of Joy*

Mom could hardly wait for the stores to open after Christmas so she could buy some baby necessities. "Can you cover for me an hour or two while the baby's sleeping, Bill? Phillip and I will do some shopping for baby things and I'll need some groceries if we're going to have company."

Dad winked, "I think I can remember how to handle this task. She seems to be a very easy-going baby. If she makes a really nasty mess in her pants I'll leave it until you get home," he teased, winking at Phillip again.

By Tuesday when out-of-towners began arriving to see the baby, Mom had most everything under control. She hadn't needed to purchase many things for Laura because when the news had spread to friends at church, she learned that the young mothers' circle would be having a baby shower. Judy Boyd, whose doctor husband worked at the same offices as my dad, was also planning a shower. Hal and Judy had been at the hospital to comfort my parents on the night I died. I think they were especially ready to help out whenever they could because they had a little boy named

Chris who was almost my same age and they knew they'd be very sad if he ever died.

Auntie Alice's family and Granny arrived on Tuesday with baby presents wrapped in big pink ribbons. They brought more pajamas and bibs, a frilly dress with a bonnet, and an inflatable blue bathtub that looked like a minature rubber raft. Phillip showed off his toy train set, but the cousins were more interested in the new baby. Since everyone wanted to hold her, Phillip got the clock from his bedroom and timed the holding sessions. "Three minutes," he said, "then pass her on." All the boys and men took turns, even Uncle Maynard, but they agreed to hand Laura off to Auntie Alice when she made a stinky diaper.

When the baby burped, the four boys had a contest to see who could burp the loudest. Mom raised her eyebrows as a signal for Phillip to stop such bad manners, but it was no use. They burped up a real chorus and got to laughing so hard they rolled on the floor.

As Uncle Alex watched the action from Heaven he admitted he was partially to blame for the burping. "When I was alive and spending time with Alice's boys, loud burping was always a way to get us in a funny mood. We all knew better than to do it out in public, but it didn't matter when we were just goofing around at home. I was pretty famous for being a jokester. When I managed my gut truck, my customers knew they could count on me to have a fresh joke every single day."

"You had a truck full of guts?" I asked.

"No, no," Unk laughed. "Don't you remember the lunch wagon I drove around Seattle to serve food to workers in the south end? That was called a 'gut' truck. Auntie Ginny and I had a route with six breakfast stops in the morning – places like the leather glove factory and the Boeing parking lot. We opened up the back of the truck and served coffee and sweet rolls, but also a waffle, bacon and egg sandwich we'd developed. Back before the hamburger places started serving fast food in the morning it was a big seller and we had a good business. It meant we were up every morning by 4:30 a.m. and greeting customers by six, so I made a point of bringing laughter into their early morning lives to help them get the day started off right. By 10:30 we circled back to the start of the route, ready to serve lunch food at the six sites. I think some of the regulars came more to hear my joke of the day than to buy food."

"I think Auntie Alice took over and became the best joker and kidder in the family after you died," I recalled. "She's really fun. My dad is funny, too. He can imitate almost anyone, like Howard Cosell, Julia Child, or Lawrence Welk's 'Turn-a off-a the bubble machine!'"

We looked down to see that Auntie Alice was not joking now. She got all teary as she held the baby. "I never had a chance to hold Phillip and Scotty when they were tiny because you lived in New Mexico. I'm going to spoil this baby girl rotten," she warned. "Thank you for giving me this beautiful new niece."

Everyone who saw Laura thought she was beautiful. She had so much hair it had to be combed and tamed. Mom went right out and bought some pastel-colored barrettes with little animals on them. Dad called them "hair do-dads" and teased about how "foo-foo" and frilly the house was becoming. Laura's complexion was almost tan and her eyes were a deep brown, like Mom's. Phillip and I both had blue eyes like Daddy. Even more than her physical beauty, people remarked on how calm and happy Laura was most of the time. She had a wide-awake period from 10 p.m. until after midnight, but by the time she was two weeks old she slept through until morning.

After the Rose Bowl game and New Years, my dad went back to working long days and Phillip returned to first grade bragging that he got the best Christmas present of all, a new baby sister. Mom kept busy with all the care Laura required, and she was loving it. My friends in Heaven were happy about the new Mayhall baby, especially Uncle Bob.

"Scotty," he reminded me, "you were going to tell me more about you and your family during the time you were on Earth. I bet your mom really loved bathing and feeding and rocking you, just like she's enjoying this time with your new baby sister."

"Oh yeah," I recalled, "Steve wants to hear more about my earth life, too. I'll ask Uncle Alex to join us because he can help me remember the times when I was really little. Phillip and I loved to look at my mom's picture albums with her little diary notes, and that's mostly how I know what I looked like and what our family was doing when I was a baby and toddler."

"Why don't we gather in the treehouse this afternoon to share some of those memories?" suggested Uncle Bob. " I'll see if Helen and GG want to come along. Maybe one of them will bring some snacks to munch on as we reminisce."

28   Scotty's Life in New Mexico

Uncle Alex arrived at the treehouse first, just as Uncle Bob and Helen were making their way across their back yard. She carried a big bag of popcorn balls which she tossed up to Unk. She slipped out of her grandma shoes to climb the rope ladder with help from Uncle Bob. Unk told me later about the memories the three of them shared before the rest of us arrived.

"We love to hear these little ones relate their memories of life on Earth," said Bob. "Even though they were there for just a short time, knowing about their families, pets and hometowns enriches my love and understanding for each one. Alex, you probably have some personal memories to add since Cheron was your sister as well as Scotty's mother."

"Oh, yes," smiled Unk, "I still remember the phone conversation I had with Cheron and Bill right after Scotty was born. Cheron told me she had timed it so that delivery would be soon after their arrival at the hospital. But then the doctor discovered the baby was out of position and needed to do a flip before being born. He advised Cheron to put up with the labor pains a while longer because he was almost certain the baby would roll over naturally without him having to use forceps. I had to laugh as Cheron described how streams of medical students and doctors-in-training came by to watch for the flip, all the while she was propped in the stirrups and huffing and puffing to get through the contractions. I guess that's part of being a patient in a medical school hospital. You don't get much privacy. She told how a cheer went up when the group at the end of the bed watched the top of the baby's head rotate into position. By that time she didn't care who was watching, just so she could now push and get the birthing over and done with.

"Scotty was born strong and healthy only four hours after Cheron was admitted to the hospital. She told Ginny and me that it went better than the night two years earlier when Phillip was born in the same hospital. She had worked steadily as a medical social worker right up to her due date. It was her first baby and she didn't perceive that she was in labor that evening when she served tacos and Nehi orange soda for dinner. When Bill took her to the hospital about 10 p.m. Phillip still wasn't ready to be born for many hours. Bill stuck with Cheron as LaMaze coach, helping her to breath and be comfortable. She rewarded him by throwing up her colorful dinner all over his pants and shirt. The nurses got the mess mopped up and brought Bill a green outfit from the operating room." Uncle Bob and Helen burst into laughter.

About this time, the rest of us were arriving at the treehouse. GG brought a plate of snickerdoodles. Steve and I had invited Esther and Lila who shared a bedroom next to ours in GG's house. They were our favorite girls because they liked playing with us and our Lego town better than playing with dolls. We all heard the laughter and the last part of Unk's story about my dad and the throw-up. Before we could get up to the platform, Lila scrunched up her nose and said loudly, "That musta been pretty yucky. The worst thing I ever threw up was pizza and birthday cake after my party at Chuck E. Cheese. It had all this red stuff and green stuff in it…"

GG interrupted and changed the subject quickly, hoping to avoid more of the kids' throw-up reports. "What a lovely afternoon beneath the branches of this big shade tree. Is everyone comfortable?"

Steve, who had been waiting a long time for my storytelling, got everyone arranged in a circle, with the grown-ups placed so they could lean against a branch or the side of the treehouse. He had told me how his own grandma always needed a backrest because of her "sacroiliac." We loved that funny word, even though we didn't know what it meant. Houdini the cat climbed down from the higher branches to curl up in Helen's lap. Then all eyes were on me. I'd told Unk and GG they'd need to help me remembering when I was a baby because I only knew what I'd heard my parents say or what was written under the pictures in the albums Mom made. Phillip and I had spent hours with those albums and he was proud that he could read her notes.

"Well," I began, " I know I was born at Bernalillo County Medical Center hospital in Albuquerque. Mom and Dad both worked at that hospital. I don't remember being born, but I can remember going to the hospital to see my doctor for appointments when I was two and our family had moved back to the city from Truth or Consequences in the desert.

Three mornings a week Mom and I drove Phillip to preschool at the Congregational church next to the hospital. Phillip was very smart and proud because he could say the whole name, 'Bernalillo County Medical Center,' but everyone else called it BCMC for short."

GG shared her memory of a story about what happened when I got home from the hospital and my granny, her daughter, came to help Mom. "She flew into Albuquerue from Seattle and rented a car. She helped Cheron with changing, feeding and rocking two little boys. She especially enjoyed conversations with Phillip since he had just become a talker at age two. She played lots of games with Phillip to keep him busy so Scotty and Cheron could nap. When she got ready to fly back home her car keys were nowhere to be found. She had allowed Phillip to play with them and now the keys had disappeared from the face of the earth. They looked through the toy box and in every square inch of the house but the keys never turned up. The rental car company came to the rescue, but it continued a mystery what had happened to the keys. Phillip may have flushed them down the toilet or dropped them down a heater vent, but he wasn't telling."

Now I was remembering the picture albums and shots of me when I was bald and very small. There were lots of photos of Phillip because he loved to cuddle close to Mom and Dad when I was getting a bottle. He liked to wind up all my new toys that made music and he kept rubbing my head to see if I was growing more fuzz on top. I told my treehouse audience, "When I was three months old we moved to Truth or Consequences, New Mexico, so Dad could work a year at the children's hospital there. That was a good year because Mom stayed home, except for working as the Weight Watchers director and doing interviews to help one of the doctors with a research project. Mom got real thin and she had plenty of time to make clothes for us with her sewing machine.

"The other young doctors working there, from New Mexico, Oklahoma and Colorado, had many little kids, mostly boys. We spent a lot of time at the hospital swimming pool because the weather was so hot. We got together for meals and play times almost every day because the town was very small and there wasn't much else to do." I could tell from the photos that I really loved the water and could almost swim with floaties on my arms.

"The next year Dad worked six months in Albuquerque and six months in Gallup. Mom went to two colleges in the city to take classes so she could get into graduate school later. In Gallup she got a full-time job as a career counselor for high schools on the Indian reservations. Dad told me two stories from that time: Phillip and I went to a babysitter's where we were playing Superman one day and Phillip split his ear open trying to fly off the ledge of the fireplace. There was lots of blood; Phillip had to have his ear sewn up and it left a scar. The other thing was about Mom getting hepatitis. She turned yellow but Dad just thought she had a good tan because he's colorblind. When she fainted making dinner one evening he took a good look and saw that the whites of her eyes were tanned too. After she got better, Dad came down with hepatitis the day he was to report for National Guard duty at a hospital in El Paso. Ended up he spent his two weeks of duty in the military hospital as a patient rather than a doctor."

I could remember for real when we packed up all our furniture in a U-Haul truck and drove from New Mexico to Salem, Oregon. I told the gang in Uncle Bob's treehouse, "Dad had spent the spring and winter looking for towns where he could open up an office to do his doctor work. Mom wanted to settle in a place where she could drive to a college to study counseling. We could have moved to Reno or San Francisco, but Dad preferred Oregon and Mom liked the idea of a smaller town rather than a big city. Anyhow, we drove the truck with the Volkswagen camper van attached behind. Our dog, Sonya, rode in the van because there was only room for the four of us in the truck cab. We arrived at our new house in the forest outside Salem on July fourth.

"Sonya was happy as a puppy to run around the big, wooded yard. Phillip and I each had our own rooms. The downstairs part was not finished at all. It was just a huge room with a cement floor. When the rains started that fall, we took our tricycles and big toys down there to play where it was dry and we wouldn't be tracking mud into the house from the yard and driveway." That was about all Unk and I could remember about my babyhood. I had already told my heavenly friends about my life after the move to Oregon. Steve and Uncle Bob thanked Unk and me for sharing these remembrances while the snickerdoodles and popcorn balls were passed around.

29 Laura Makes the Rounds

One of the secretaries at Dad's office was a wonderful artist. She offered to make a special birth announcement for Laura. She drew a picture of Phillip, Heidi, and our gray cat, Sargeant Pepper, beside the rocking cradle Granddaddy made. Baby Laura was in the cradle and a little Christmas tree stood behind them. Above their heads was a banner held by butterflies with the words, "A most blessed event." Mom wrote a poem for the inside:

> She came to us on Christmas day, a wondrous gift so fair.
> Beneath our little tree she lay to banish our despair.
> We'd hoped this holiday season to find new joy and peace,
> So let us share the reason our joy will now increase:
>
> Laura Belinda Joy Mayhall
> Born December 23, 1977
> Weight 8 lbs., 1 oz.; Length 20 inches
> Lots of dark brown hair and dark eyes
> Proud and joyful adoptive family:
> Bill, Cheron, Phillip, Heidi-pie and Sargeant Pepper

Even before the announcements were in the mail, droves of people started visiting and calling. Every day people brought baby gifts, including the mailman who delivered packages most mornings. After the two baby showers there wasn't enough room in the nursery to store all the gifts coming Laura's way. Three people brought big boxes of hand-me-downs from their girl babies. One was Mom's sorority sister, Sue, who had three daughters and lived near Portland. "Well, we'll just have to change her clothes several times a day to show off all these darling outfits," exclaimed my mom. You could tell she enjoyed dressing Laura in all the tiny, frilly, soft clothing. She let Phillip select a favorite dress or romper each morning before he left for school. I think he was a little embarrassed to realize how much he enjoyed dressing his baby-doll sister.

It was obvious to my parents that their friends were relieved and much more relaxed now that their visits and conversations centered on Laura. The house didn't feel so lonely and sad because of my absence. Mom's days were suddenly very full and she had to plan carefully in order to save a day or two a week for her research project. A neighbor down the road was thrilled to offer childcare for Laura most Tuesdays and Thursdays while Phillip was in school and Mom had some quiet time to study at home or at the library.

On her first trip to confer with her major professor at OSU in Corvallis, Mom took the baby dressed in a ruffly green outfit that complemented Laura's complexion and eyes. She didn't tell anyone the baby was coming, which pretty much wrecked everyone's concentration for the afternoon. She was passed around among all the adoring professors and graduate students. She never cried one bit and they all seemed happy to put aside their reading or stop correcting papers. After leaving campus Mom swung by Little Beavers where there were a half dozen young teachers and thirty preschoolers all wanting to get their hands on Laura. Some of them had baby sisters or brothers at home so they knew how to hold her head up and coo to her. Some of the kids remembered me and said they were happy to meet "Scotty's baby sister." I had proud feelings when I heard that, even though I was in Heaven and couldn't rock Baby Laura myself.

When she was thirteen days old, Mom took Laura to Phillip's school for show-and-tell. The teacher held the baby up in front of the class so Phillip could tell his story about getting her at the lawyer's office on Christmas day. He bragged about how he could test the bottle to be sure the milk was just warm enough before feeding her. He liked rocking Laura in the cradle but not being in the same room when Mom changed a dirty diaper. He got real theatrical, holding his nose and shouting, "peee-you!".

The doctors' wives who had formed a tennis group to get Mom

out of the house and exercising every Friday picked up where they'd left off before the holidays and the blessed event. The second Friday in January they were back on the courts playing doubles. Now Laura became the mascot not only for these four but for all the women who played regularly at the Courthouse. Mom propped her up in her baby chair off to the side where she could see the action. Everyone remarked what a good baby she was because she almost never cried or fussed.

Having a baby in the family was like medicine to help with the healing. There was much more happiness and energy in our house. Grieving was on the back burner most of the time. Mom had a couple of memorial projects she wanted to complete, but these she could handle without falling apart and crying. Memories of me were becoming sweeter rather than always stinging so painfully.

The national Compassionate Friends organization was selling a beautiful print for a fundraiser. Mom got permission to use it in the creation of a children's play area in the waiting room at Dad's office. She framed the drawing of a young boy who she thought looked a lot like me. He was dressed in blue shorts and a yellow tee-shirt, much as I'd been dressed when the accident happened and I ended up in Heaven. The background looked like drapes of blue fabric and the boy was smiling happily as he watched a golden butterfly dancing above his head. The little boy looked happy. Mom thought of me with warmth and happiness when she looked at the picture.

Mom and Dad's tenth anniversary happened in late December, right after Christmas and Laura's coming into the family. Mom decided to make a collage of family pictures to capture the decade, starting with their wedding-day photo and ending with a snapshot of their new family for 1978, in which Baby Laura was the central focus. Of course, there were lots of pictures of Phillip and me as babies and toddlers, as well as Sonya our "shusky" dog, Sargeant Pepper the cat, and Heidi-pie.

Many weekends during the winter months my family would

drive around the county trying to find some Western items for the memorial playground at Little Beavers. They hoped to buy a covered wagon that kids could climb, and some old wagon wheels to decorate the play yard. They ended up with a buckboard and some additional wheels that were probably a hundred years old. Dad liked to fix things and set to work repairing any damage and making everything safe for kids to play on. Dad also started clearing and preparing an area in the garage where he could build the space capsule Granddaddy had designed. Though I had liked playing cowboys with my Little Beavers friends, I was really happy they'd have this spaceship so they could pretend to take voyages with Captain Kirk and his Star Trek crew. I figured if I wished real hard and made the love link between Heaven and Little Beavers, I could join the fun. Instead of "Beam me up, Scotty" they'd be beaming me down!

30 Valentine's Day

Mom planned to visit my grave on Valentine's day in February. It began snowing the morning of the fourteenth so Mom bundled Laura in a snowsuit and warm blankets. The roads were clear of snow and ice by mid-afternoon, but the cemetery was blanketed by several inches of whiteness. Mom had difficulty finding the roadways leading to the section where I was buried. She left the motor running to keep Laura and the interior of the car warm. Armed with a wreath she'd made of red silk rosebuds, she stepped out into the snow, wishing she'd thought to wear gloves and boots instead of slip-on shoes. With cold, wet feet she searched the area for my grave, disoriented by the white-out conditions of the ground. Only a few markers extended above the snow and she began to panic and cry. Later she told Dad, "I had this overwhelming feeling that I'd lost Scotty beyond all hope of staying connected. I brushed snow off the flat stones I could locate by touch. My hands and fingers were freezing. I couldn't stop crying and I felt so wretched I thought I might vomit. Finally I came to the stone I knew covered the grave next to Scotty's. I was finally able to leave the wreath and say a prayer for Scotty, and for all of us who have broken hearts for the pain of missing our beloved child on Valentine's Day."

When she got home she dug through her "thought file" which had been inspired by Mr. Wettleson – Uncle Bob. She remembered having filed away a poem printed on one of the condolence cards they'd received months before. Reading it again and again, she came to terms with the emotions of the day and felt some relief from her sorrow.

> Do not stand at my grave and weep,
> I am not there, I do not sleep.
> I am a thousand winds that blow;
> I am the diamond glint on snow.
> I am the sunlight on ripened grain;
> I am the gentle autumn rain.
>
> When you wake in the morning hush
> I am the swift uplifting rush
> of quiet birds in circling flight.
> I am the soft starlight at night.
> Do not stand at my grave and weep,
> I am not there, I do not sleep.
> – *Hopi Indian Prayer*

31 Lunch with Albert

One morning after breakfast, while I was sitting in GG's porch swing, Uncle Bob called to me from the raspberry patch in his front yard. "Come taste some of these sweet berries, Scotty. I want to tell you something."

As I stuffed my mouth with the juicy berries, Uncle Bob told me that he and Helen had invited the Schweitzers for lunch a few days later. "Because your mom has told you about the life and work of Albert and Helene, I thought you might like to meet them for yourself."

"My mom told Phillip and me she had wanted to travel to Africa to meet Dr. Schweitzer, but he died and went to Heaven before she got back from the Peace Corps. Sure, I would love to have lunch at your house and meet them. I'll ask GG if it's okay."

GG told me it was an honor to meet the Schweitzers. "Even though every one of us is equally precious to God the Father, we are aware of how famous Dr. Schweitzer became for all his good works on Earth. He is very smart and also very proper. You will need to remember your best manners and always say, 'Yes, sir,' 'Thank you, ma'm.' And don't interrupt when he or Helene is talking, okay?"

"Yeah, I can do that," I replied. "We didn't talk like that much in our family, but I remember how my uncle David, Dad's brother, talked that way. I think that's the way Grandmother and Granddaddy in Texas raised their sons to speak. I will say 'sir' and 'ma'm' when I speak to the Schweitzers, just like Uncle David talked."

Uncle Bob had some advice for me, too. "You probably remember in the storybooks about Albert that he believed in 'reverence for life.' Do you remember what that means, Scotty?"

"It means don't kill, and to take care of all living things," I recalled. "Mom told us it was a good way to live, except it was okay to kill some bugs or snakes or mean animals if they were hurting others. When our dogs got fleas we killed them with flea medicine. When aphids chewed up Mom's roses she got ladybugs to eat them, but the ladybugs all flew away so she used a poison spray. I won't tell Albert Schweitzer she did that."

"I think that would be wise," Uncle Bob said with a smile. "Three of the teens – Jacques, Payam and Su Ling – have asked to eat lunch with the Schweitzers, too. They are interested in religion and philosophy, organ music and hearing about nursing and medical missions. That means there will be eight of us around the dining table so we'll all have to be good, patient listeners."

"I know not to talk with my mouth full," I assured him. " Can I talk after I swallow my food?"

"Of course. Let me suggest you think up two or three questions you would most like to ask. I will see that you get to sit next to Helene so you won't be forgotten at the other end of the table."

The morning before the luncheon I combed my hair and slipped into my cowboy boots. I even decided to wear my belts with some of my emergency equipment attached. I knew Dr. Schweitzer would like to see my stethoscope and the elastic bandages and tape Dad gave me to use in case one of my friends got a pretend injury. I left the gun I'd made from a piece of maple tree on the end of my bed because of "reverence for life." I didn't want him to think I'd kill an animal or a person. I decided not to wear my plastic fireman hat but wished I had a pith helmet like the one Albert always wore at his jungle hospital.

GG sent a booster chair next door because I was going to be awfully short among all those grown-ups and teenagers around the table. The centerpiece decoration was a cluster of wooden animal figures from Africa. One of Uncle Bob's former students from the Franklin High journalism club had brought this gift when he returned from covering a news story in the Congo. Along with his big library full of books, this gift was one of Uncle Bob's prized possessions. That's why he had chosen to have it in Heaven with them. All the foods were on the table in covered dishes so our group could pass them around and eat family style. Helen had prepared some of the things the Schweitzers liked best because they reminded them of Africa: crunchy brown rice, sweet potatoes without marshmallows, black beans, lemonade, and tapioca pudding topped with raspberries for dessert.

After saying a blessing over the food, everyone dished up their plates and ate with very good manners. I remembered to put my napkin in my lap. Su Ling was the first kid to speak because she was a girl and the rest of us were boys. She told all of us how she had planned to be a nurse when she grew up. She would have loved to do nurse work like Helene in the jungle. "But no one gets sick or injured in Heaven, so I'm wondering what other work I can find to do?" she queried.

Helene Schweitzer was pleased to address this question. "Even more important than dressing wounds or giving shots, a nurse needs to give comfort to the spirit. A nurse must be able to help heal more than the physical body. You are nursing when you care lovingly for little chidren or take the time to talk with the old ones who sometimes get very lonely, even here in Heaven. They like to have stories read to them. So, I understand you spend lots of time each day reading to others, Su Ling. That is a marvelous way to provide comfort and joy, just like a nurse would."

The Wettlesons were proud as they listened to the other teens pose their questions then discuss answers with Albert and Helene. It was all very interesting, but I started getting worried there wouldn't be time for my questions. Finally Albert looked right at me, asking about my equipment. "Scotty, tell me about that stethoscope dangling from your belt."

"Yes, sir, Dr. Schweitzer. Thank you for asking, Dr. Schweitzer. Did you know that my dad's a doctor down in Oregon? I liked to pretend I was a doctor and paramedic so my friend, Dr. Chester, gave me this stethoscope. Dad never had patients in Africa or in a jungle, just regular people like we had in New Mexico and Oregon. Sometimes my brother Phillip and I went with him on rounds at the hospital on Saturday mornings. People told us he was a wonderful doctor. He didn't play the organ like you, though. He played the French horn in the Texas marching band for a while. Dad doesn't really like organ music. He goes to church for Pastor Ed's sermons but he complains about all the standing up, sitting down and slow music played by the organist or sung by the choir."

Albert Schweitzer and the others chuckled. "Well, little one, I'll have to think of a special concert of more lively music to play for your dad when he joins us here in Heaven. How would that be?"

"I'd like that, sir. Maybe Mom and Phillip will be here too. We can go as a family like we used to. And Baby Laura, my new sister." I moved on to my second question. "I was wondering if you ever met Jesus. I met him in the meadow with John the Baptist and they told us wonderful stories from the Bible. My best friend, Steve, gave Jesus his birdhouse and I made Him a walking stick."

"Yes, Helene and I have had the pleasure of meeting Jesus several times. Three times He's come to my organ concerts and we feel so honored. Jesus told me He loves music and I have played a few lively tunes for Him, too. Some of the rhythms I adapted from the music of the jungle sound a lot like what He'd heard at celebrations in Jerusalem and Gallilee long ago. I feel humble and blessed to play for Him. By the way, we have also met the Dalai Lama, Ghandi, Martin Luther, Martin Luther King, Jr., Helen Keller, Eleanor Roosevelt and Dag Hammarskjold. I have a keen interest in talking with others who lived lives of peace and tried to bring justice to the people on Earth."

"You look a little perplexed, Scotty," said Helene. "Are you wondering, 'Who are all these people Albert is talking about?'"

"Well, ma'm, I was thinking that people with last names like Lama, Ghandi and Hammarskjold probably aren't American and don't speak English. Excuse me, but I don't understand how Albert can have long conversations with them."

I could tell Albert was enjoying my questions, just like Rhonda, my teacher at Little Beavers, always liked them. Albert had wonderful hands that had grown strong from all those years of doctoring, hospital building and organ playing. I remembered Mom had said he lived to be 90 years old. Now he folded his old hands across his chest and leaned back in his chair to answer my last question.

"In Heaven, language is not a barrier. We can learn to speak and understand other languages easily if we really want to. In the Christian Bible there is reference to this happening at the celebration of Pentecost."

"Oh, I get it, sir. It's like the first day when I arrived in Heaven I became a reader just like magic because that's one of the things I most wanted to learn when I was on Earth."

"Exactly," said Albert. "In addition, here in Heaven we can receive and understand what others say in whatever language they're speaking, even though we might never have heard that language before. For example, Jacques here speaks in French. Helene and I know both French and German so there's no need for translation. But the rest of you probably don't understand French, yet you understood perfectly well his questions and the conversation we had. Payam's language is Farsi; Su Ling's is Chinese, Mandarin."

Uncle Bob added, "Over at your great-grandmother's house next door, Jesus and Gilberto speak Spanish, while Sasha speaks Russian. Esther's language is Hebrew. Did you realize that, Scotty?"

"No," I giggled, a little embarrassed. "I just thought we were all speaking English all this time! This is so cool, to be able to understand all the languages of all the people of the world – 'red and yellow, black and white' – all the languages are precious in Jesus' sight, just like all the little children are."

That was one of the most wonderful afternoons I ever spent in Heaven or on Earth. I felt special to be included along with the teenagers who were so smart and well-behaved. While I had always loved spending time talking with Uncle Bob and Helen, the hours with Albert and Helene Schweitzer filled me with wonder and made me feel very grown up. It was quite a while before I got to my first organ concert to hear Albert play. Uncle Bob had told him I would be in the audience and, you know what? He played two pieces just for me: "Miss Merry Mac" and "Jesus Loves the Little Children." Then he gave me a pith helmet, just my size!

32 Rhonda and Remembrance

Most of Mom's spare time was now devoted to studying for tests and preparing her research. She had to take both written and oral comprehensive exams to demonstrate to her professors that she'd learned enough in her doctoral studies to be a good professional counselor. These exams were scheduled for May, 1978. She also had a number of meetings with her advisor and committee to tie down the subject and procedures for her doctoral project and dissertation. Though she would really have preferred to delay all this and just concentrate on mothering, she never liked to leave tasks unfinished. Besides, it was a good diversion and intellectual challenge which helped her healing after losing me. This was especially true, now, since she had convinced the professors to let her study parents' recovery after the sudden death of a small child. She intended to interview members of The Compassionate Friends organizations in the Willamette Valley. She believed she could approach it in a way that would be beneficial to both interviewer and interviewees. Also, the published research paper could be useful in future years for other bereaved parents and the professionals who try to help mourners through the grieving process.

One day in early March, Rhonda, my former teacher, called Mom to set up a visit on my birthday, March 13. Rhonda had gotten married and wasn't teaching at the preschool anymore, but she said she'd saved some things from my school folder which she wanted to bring for Mom and Dad to have. Mom loved Rhonda and knew it would be a good way to spend part of the sad day when I would have been five years old if I was still on Earth.

After greeting with hugs and tears, then getting Laura settled in her crib for a nap, they sat with cups of tea in the family room. Rhonda reminisced: "I loved how Scotty called me 'Wanda.' I always knew when I heard him call my name that I was in for a treat or a challenge. In almost every way he was ahead of the other kids in my three- and four-year-old class. In fact, I grew to depend on Scotty to be a leader and help me with the others, especially when we broke into smaller groups. He could learn a skill or concept quickly, so he could be teaching it to some of the others, helping me with the teaching."

Rhonda spread my report cards on the coffee table and pointed out some of her written observations: "Very positive attitude toward school." "Anxious and quick to learn; asserts independence." "Driven by a desire to complete all tasks well." "Sensitive and very loving toward special friends." "Self-help skills way ahead of schedule." I recalled that I was toilet trained even before we moved from New Mexico, but a few of the kids in Rhonda's class still wet their pants or needed someone to take them to the bathroom so they didn't have accidents. I learned to tie my shoes when Dad and Mom were working so hard to teach Phillip. So, I could help my Little Beavers friends with their tie-up shoes when we finished nap time and were headed to play outside. I usually wore my cowboy boots so I could slip into them very fast.

"I know his desire to keep up with Phillip was strong," Mom told Rhonda. "Actually, he seemed to learn most things easier than Phillip, except for reading. He wanted so much to be a reader."

"He certainly loved our circle times when I read them stories. He had an excellent memory. He'd mastered all the long names of dinosaurs and was beginning to recognize them as spelled words. Of course, he knew all his letters and could read everyone's nametag. He loved writing the alphabet. He knew to always start left-to-right and he formed each letter with good control and exactness.

"Scotty was always interested in how things worked and how they went together," Rhonda continued. "We got an old adding machine to help us learn our numbers. It required many sequential steps to create the paper tape and see the numbers come up in the right order. He was fascinated by that sort of thing; he seemed mechanically inventive. He also loved our cooking sessions. He could slice, chop and mix with precision. He would say, 'I can make it myself!'" She chuckled. "One day in June when we were cutting strawberries he delighted me as he used knife and fork in the correct fashion, saying, 'This is the way my mom uses her knife and fork.' All his fine motor skills were well developed. He enjoyed working with scissors, pencils, crayons, puzzles, Legos, painting, building blocks, water-table play and the sandbox."

"Well, I know Scotty wasn't perfect, but he sure had a lot going for him," Mom concurred. "He especially looked forward to field trips, seeing and learning new things. But I remember he was sometimes a handful. I see your notes about this, right here. "

Rhonda reviewed her handwriting on the report card. "Just overexcitement, which I was delighted to see, but I sometimes needed to restrain him from running off ahead of the group. A few times, early in the year, we dealt with his angry outbursts, but he settled down rapidly when we tried to talk it out. The behavior soon subsided. Scotty was always aware when he was doing something wrong. He accepted the consequences for bad behavior very well.

"He excelled in large-motor play both indoors and out. He could run, skip and jump in those cowboy boots of his. He developed secret hide-outs in the play yard and invited his best friends, like Adrian, Justin and Jarrett, to join him there for their own games. When we went to play in the big gym at the university, Scotty especially loved the ropes. That child could use ropes in the most creative ways. For example, he'd tie two or three of the tricycles together so they could ride in tandem, or he'd attach a rope to one of the larger pieces of equipment so he and a group of his friends could pull it across the hardwood floor to where they wanted it. Maybe they'd be setting up a fort to play cowboys and Indians. Scotty was such a character, I loved to watch him role playing. One of his favorites was acting the parts of TV characters or pretending he was 'Dr. Mayhall.'

"When Scotty started winking and whistling it cracked me up,"

Rhonda said with a smile. "He became a bit of a flirt. Where did that come from?"

"That would be his twin cousins, David and Danny," Mom recalled. "They visited us over spring break. When Scotty imitated one of them by whistling for the first time, they helped him learn to call Heidi that way. Being teenagers interested in girls, they encouraged him to develop a wolf whistle he could use with all the pretty girls. If he winked and whistled at you, Rhonda, consider yourself one of Scotty's 'pretty girls'."

All this remembering was getting to be too much for Mom and she couldn't help crying. Rhonda cried, too. "Many people have told me, 'God only takes the best and brightest...,' trying to make me feel better about losing Scotty, I guess. If that's the case, God sure got a good one when I lost my little boy." She choked on her words. "It's just hard to accept that the timing was right. We wanted and expected to have Scotty grow up here on Earth, then God would have his turn after Scotty had had a chance to live a full life. It's just so out of order for à child to die before his parents. He was so little."

Mom thanked Ronda for sharing this afternoon of memories and the report cards. She had chosen one of Scotty's drawings as a gift and had it framed for Rhonda. It portrayed Scotty and some of his class friends in stick figures, with Rhonda's circle face in the middle grinning from ear to ear at her charges. "It's precious," she said with a thankful hug. "I will cherish it always, as I will Scotty's memory."

As Rhonda drove down the driveway and out of sight, Mom gathered a small bouquet of daffodils from the yard. These came up from the bulbs I had helped her plant that last autumn. She had decided to use them in a memorial bouquet on the altar at church on the Sunday closest to my birthday each year. Every year after that she added one big yellow daffodil to the bouquet of ivy and baby's breath, starting with five daffodils in 1978. The bouquets grew larger and more lovely with each passing year. It helped people at our church remember me forever after.

33 More Tragedy on 99W

The Compassionate Friends chapter continued to grow and Mom became president. Dad went to a couple of the potlucks, but mostly this was a group of friends with whom Mom shared support. One of the families, whose beautiful adult daughter had been killed in an auto accident, had an artist in their rural community draw a large portrait of her. Her name was Denise. Mom took one of her favorite photos of me, in which I was wearing a necktie and a red sweater vest knitted by my Grandmother Mayhall, for the artist to do a 15" x 20" sketch in pastels. It hung on the wall above our piano for years, joined eventually by portraits of Grandmother and Granddaddy after they'd died from old age in the 1990s.

Mom developed a workshop she presented around Oregon and at The Compassionate Friends regional conference in California, using the information she had learned from her counseling and research work, as well as personal experience. She wrote articles for some newsletters, all of which seemed to help other parents and to give her comfort in knowing she could assist them through their grief.

It was while Mom was Compassionate Friends president that another accident happened in the very same spot where I'd been killed. A van filled with college students traveling between campuses was struck and demolished. The highway department decided it was time to install a traffic light. Mom wrote a letter to the editor of the newspaper, entitled "Death on the Highway."

> I guess one small dead boy is not a very impressive statistic. That's how it seemed when our son Scotty was killed in an auto accident on Highway 99W.
>
> We frantically searched for answers to why this

tragedy had happened. We pleaded with law enforcement officers to improve traffic conditions and make that stretch of highway safer for motorists. But we were repeatedly assured that the signs and markings were adequate…and no improvements were made.

Now, within the span of 28 hours, seven women have lost their lives near this treacherous intersection and another died later. I deplore this senseless loss of human life, and weep with the families who mourn for their loved ones.

When tragedies such as this occur – especially when a child is killed – the survivors are overcome with feelings of helplessness and futility. It is important in working through their grief that they find some way to make sense of the situation or to prevent such an awful thing from happening again. When all efforts to do so are thwarted, it is a far greater task to resolve the feelings of anger and guilt that complicate and prolong the process.

Today it feels like a very hollow victory, indeed, that the much overdue traffic light will soon be installed. I hope the families of these recent victims will find some small measure of satisfaction and comfort in knowing that these deaths have not gone unnoticed. But what a dreadful price to pay!

(Cheron Mayhall, President, Salem area chapter, The Compassionate Friends)

34 Baptism and Birthday

As spring weather and longer daylight hours arrived in the Northwest, traveling became easier so friends and family came to visit almost every weekend. All the aunts, uncles, cousins and Granny from Washington state dropped in to get acquainted with Laura and to see for themselves just how well my family was doing after I'd been dead for nine months. Two carloads of Mom's college friends came and they had a great reunion at our house. One of them was the sorority sister Mom had named Laura after. Also in this group were two of Mom's college boyfriends, Jim and David. Dad always kidded her about how she managed to stay in touch with these guys.

"Well," she told him, "it's hard for me to just let go of people who have shared my life and love, even if they are 'old boyfriends.' They were very dear to me back then, and now you and I have them, and their wives too, in our circle of friends. Don't worry, honey," she teased, "it could be worse. You don't even know the two college guys I was engaged to. I thought I was madly in love with them and hoped to be married, but they both dumped me and broke my heart. I tried to establish contact when I got over it, but they didn't reciprocate. Anyhow, it's you who won my affection and devotion in the end. Consider yourself the lucky one! I do. It's all worked out for the best."

My parents decided to have Laura baptized the day before Phillip's birthday in mid-April so that Granny and Auntie Alice's family could come for both occasions. The afternoon I was telling Steve about the planned christening he almost burst his buttons with the news that his mom was going to have a baby. "My mom and dad took my two sisters and our dachshund, Carbie, for a walk on the beach," he recounted with excitement. "She told the girls her wonderful news about the baby growing in her tummy. Lori and Karen were so happy they started turning cartwheels on the sand. Carbie raced around and yipped. Then they praised God for this gift of another child on the way. I concentrated real hard to make the love link and I'm just sure they felt my spirit in their praise circle, right there on the beach."

Mom dressed Laura in a white knit dress for the baptism at church. She wore those rhumba pants with ruffles on the back over her diaper. She had black patent leather shoes and ruffly socks. She kept pulling the pink bow out of her hair, so Mom gave up on it.

Art and Sue had agreed to be godparents but they couldn't fly all the way from New York for the ceremony. Auntie Alice was happy to stand in for them. It all went well, Laura charming the congregation, right up until Pastor Ed took her into his arms to sprinkle the holy water on her head. At that point she let out a howling sound like none she'd ever made before. She kept on screaming so loud that no one could hear the words. Only when the pastor gave her back to Mom did she start settling down, but by then all the church folks had seen a different side of this baby they thought was so angelic and quiet. Some people thought it must have been the black clerical robe that frightened her, or maybe the water sprinkles on her head.

That same Sunday afternoon was Phillip's seventh birthday party. Granny had brought her magician friend from Seattle to perform a magic show for all the kids. Mostly Phillip got clothes and books, but his favorite gifts were the catcher's mitt and a lightweight bat made of plastic inscribed with his whole name, just like the pros. He had played a little T-ball in the fall, but now it was spring and the parks department was forming teams in each community for boys and girls of all ages. Phillip loved being part of a team, especially if they had uniforms. That continued all the way through his schooling. He never really showed much talent for sports, his specialities being spelling, reading and, later, Spanish. But he never stopped trying. Because he enjoyed the uniforms and gear so much, he always tried to convince the baseball coach to let him play catcher. That meant Mom and Dad had their hands full during the games, helping Phillip get dressed and undressed before and after every inning.

Phillip had made good progress in the academics of first grade. He could read and spell better than most of the children in his little country school, even many of the fifth graders. However, he couldn't tie his shoes. Velcro saved him from embarrassment. His printing and cursive writing were hard to read because he couldn't seem to figure out things like margins, spacing, and keeping letters the same size and in a straight line. But he had interesting things to say and write about, so Mrs. Down encouraged him despite his messy paper work. The special education teacher continued to work with Phillip in the areas where he had trouble and could get frustrated. She even helped out on the playground during recess because Phillip had problems with "gross motor skills" as well as "fine motor skills," according to his progress reports. Phillip always did well with teachers and coaches who could recognize his abilities and gifts and not get hung up on the many things he couldn't seem to master. I remembered Uncle Alex telling me about his experiences with learning disabilities…how he almost didn't graduate from high school except for some teachers who didn't give up on him. Mrs. Down helped Phillip like that.

That spring, in addition to Phillip's special needs, Mom and Dad began noticing some delays in Laura's development. Checking the notes in my baby book and Phillip's, it seemed she wasn't developing as quickly. For example, she didn't babble much and she didn't seem responsive when my parents called her name. When it was time for her to be sitting up on her own she fought it. Mom would put her on a blanket on the floor and prop her up with pillows. She seemed to hate this position and would throw herself backwards to a lying-down position. Often when Mom tried to hold her close and cuddle her head on her shoulder, Laura would push away with all her might so that Mom had trouble not dropping her. One evening when Hal and Judy Boyd had come for dinner and the grown-ups were playing pool in our basement, Dad mentioned his concerns about Laura.

"Don't worry," counseled Judy. She had a girl and two boys of her own and she knew all kids developed at different paces. "Laura is a wonderful baby and she'll be just fine." Her husband, a very smart doctor, added, "Bill, you and Cheron are probably just overprotective. That's understandable. I'd be the same if I'd lost a child. But, just look at her," he said as he glanced across to where Laura was snoozing in her wind-up swing, "she is beautiful and sweet in every way. You're doing a great job with her, so try to relax."

Mrs. Down called Mom one afternoon in May, concerned about a writing assignment Phillip had completed. She had asked the class to write about feelings. They were to recall some experience in their lives that made them especially happy or sad, angry or fearful, excited or upset. Phillip had written several pages entitled, "Death,Yeech!"

> Death, "Yeech!" I really like writing, but especially not about death. And, if you don't know why I wrote that last sentence, I'll tell you why. On March 22, 1977, I was riding in our neighbor's aunt's car, and Carla (that was her name) ran a red light, and another jerk came along and hit us!! Me and my brother, Scotty, and some of my friends, were in the car. The jerk in the other car tried to ram us!! And on the first try, CRASH!!!!!!! My friend broke one leg and one arm, and I don't know what happened to my other friend, Carla or the rest of the gang. Only I know what happened to me and Scotty. I suffered a mild concussion and a few swollen fingers. Scotty, well he suffered a hole in his lungs and then, just about five minutes later, he passed away. THE END

"Hmm," said Mom. "He hasn't got all his facts straight, but at least it's good to know he is working through his feelings about the accident. I don't think he feels guilty or unnaturally sad. Just the other day he was watching a TV show called something like 'The

Life and Times of Judge Roy Bean.' A character in the Old West, I think. He came to me and said, 'I wish they'd have a TV series called The Life and Times of Scotty Mayhall. Then he could break through the TV screen and be home again.'"

"That sounds like Phillip," Mrs. Down responded. "But I believe he is getting through all of this pretty well. He adores his baby sister and he's made many new friends at school. I'm glad he's here so I will have him in my class for another couple of years. He is a good boy who loves to read and talk, talk, talk. We'll continue giving him the opportunity to work things through. He's going to be fine."

35 Springtime

Mother's Day in May, then Father's Day in June, were a confusion of sadness and happiness because of missing me but having Laura to love and celebrate, along with Phillip. Phillip lost his first tooth about then. That seemed to make Mom sadder than anything else. She and Dad pretended to be the Tooth Fairy, taking the tooth from under Phillip's pillow after he was sound asleep, leaving in its place a shiny silver dollar. Mom told Dad a story from her childhood when she lost her first tooth. Granny had told her a fairy would come silently in the night to gather up the tooth in exchange for some coins. Mom said she obediently put the tooth beneath her pillow before falling asleep, but she was totally confused about how a ferry boat was going to get up the narrow staircase to her bedroom without crashing or making a loud noise. Water ferries crossing Puget Sound were common in the Seattle area. Once the idea of "ferry" got into Mom's head it never occurred to her that Granny was talking about a "fairy." Anyhow, what saddened Mom now was that I would never be around to lose my baby teeth and enjoy the fun of the fairy tale, just as I'd be missing out on so many growing-up milestones.

The second week in June the old grandparents came from Texas to get to know Laura. Also, Dad needed Granddaddy to help build the space capsule he'd designed for the playground. Dad had ordered all the lumber and plywood the plans specified so they got right to work in the garage. It was amazing to watch it develop, twice as tall as Daddy and big enough inside to hold a whole bunch of kids. It was shaped like the nose cone that landed in the ocean when the astronauts came back from their space flights. The whole project took almost two months from start to finish, but Granddaddy's visit got it well underway. While Grandmother enjoyed her only grandchildren and puttered in our flower beds (she was famous in the Austin Rose Society and had a rose named after her) Mom was free to help with the hammering and sawing. Grampa Larry came to help on weekends and many summer nights after Dad got home from work. Even Phillip got to help paint the capsule metallic silver when the building was finished. At the very top they placed an upside-down plastic garbage can. Mom got up on a tall ladder and painted American flags and "USS SCOTTY MAYHALL" in blue and red letters on both sides so it would be visible from the school buildings as well as from the passing highway.

    The springboard wagon in our garage was repaired and painted bright red with black, spoked wheels. Seventy-three people had donated money for the playground which was developing nicely at Little Beavers. The ground space around the two houses had been surrounded by a sturdy fence in Western, stockade style, with lookout towers on the corners. A new figure-eight asphalt track was in place for tricycles and big wheels. The swing and teeter-totter sets had a fresh coat of paint. The Easts had upgraded the outdoor crafts "corral" and the pens for our critters were refurbished. There were a few floppy-eared rabbits and more baby bunnies on the way. There was enough money in the memorial fund to purchase a sturdy Indian teepee. Dad found a dome-shaped climbing structure in a catalog. He said it looked like a molecule and reminded him of science and outer space. It went well with the space capsule, too, since the bars were bright silver and the joints were knobs of bright blue and red. All the things that could be done ahead of time were done a month before dedication day in August when they'd need a big work crew to finish the project. Dad wondered how they'd transport the capsule and wagon from our garage to the playgound, but he was always good at finding solutions to such problems.

On June 24 Mom had another one of her dreams about me. She wrote in her journal:

> It is now 11 months since Scotty's death. Last night I had a vivid dream of him, the first in quite awhile. He was back with us again. I don't recall that he did or said anything particular, but I did see him so clearly just as he was – so lovely and active. I saw him running with the dog, digging in the yard, winking, buttoning his pajamas, sleeping in his daddy's arms...
>
> In the dream, I spent a lot of time spreading the news of his return with our friends, like Satsuki and SallyJo – "It's a miracle, but he's back! Yes, I know, I saw him dead and cold, and I saw his little blue coffin at his burial, but now he's back!"
>
> I awoke feeling the warmth of his closeness, the disappointment in realizing it was only a dream, and regret for having wasted time talking to others in the dream when I might have spent those precious moments holding Scotty in my arms and loving him with all my attention. – Cheron, June 24, 1978

As the first anniversary of the accident and the completion of the playground project neared, Mom recalled with Dad and Phillip some of the images she was seeing, sometimes night dreams and sometimes day dreams. She wrote them down:

> Rolling/roughhousing on the floor of his room

Waving good-bye in front of Little Beavers with his lunch pail
Working with his "equipment" gear on the swing set in front of the house
Playing tug-o-war with Heidi-pie in the family room, giggling "You quit that! You quit that!"
Sitting on the sofa after nap time, still sleepy, frowning at the TV across the room
Chasing waves at the beach, thrilled to get "caught" by one
Playing "dead" (asleep) in the morning in his gingham-checked turquoise and white pajamas I made for him last Christmas
Dressing himself – buttons, belt, shoelaces, etc. with such efficiency and confidence

If the remembering turned sad instead of happy, it usually helped to take Laura in her arms. She'd sing and dance with the baby until her sense of gratitude and well-being returned.

36   *Deaf, Not Dead!*

July started off well. My folks had decided they needed vacation time away. They planned a camping trip to British Columbia and Alberta in Canada. They went on a car ferry up the coast to Prince Rupert, then drove east to Lake Louise and Banff Hot Springs. They did a lot of hiking. Dad seemed to love having a baby on his shoulders in the backpack. Laura was content bouncing along the trails from this vantage point, gazing at the beauty all around in the parks. The only bad experience was their run-in with swarms of mosquitos in the woods at the far end of Lake Louise. They hadn't been warned so they didn't have repellent. Covering their exposed skin they hurried back to the lodge, but they still got plenty of bites. All except Laura. Dad guessed that her blood was somehow different and not as delicious as his, Mom's and Phillip's. They went through Spokane to visit Auntie Mary's family as they headed home. It was decided that Tracy, the middle daughter who was about twelve, would ride back to Oregon to spend a couple weeks helping Mom with Laura and Phillip, thus getting a vacation herself.

It turned out to be a very good thing that Tracy was living at our house that month. Dad had made an appointment with a neurologist who could assess Laura's development and determine why she didn't want to sit up. It didn't take Dr. Schwarz very long to discover that Laura had an inner ear and balance problem. He lifted her up, gazed into her eyes, and twirled her around in circles. His diagnosis: "Why, she has no nystagmus!" He explained that meant a rapid, involuntary eye movement that should have occurred with the twirling. He predicted she'd adjust and outgrow the symptoms without intervention. As he was preparing to leave the exam room, Mom mentioned that Laura didn't seem to respond when her name was called. Dad would come home from work and call to her. No response. Mom would hear her waking and fussing down the hall after nap, but she wouldn't seem soothed by Mom's voice coming down the hall, until she actually could see Mom enter the nursery. Then she'd settle down. Dr. Schwarz picked up a small bell and crept up behind Laura where Mom held her sitting on the exam table. He rang the bell right behind her head, but she showed no recognition of the noise. "I don't think she hears," exclaimed the doctor. He told Mom to take her to the pediatrician to get this checked out.

The very next day they were in the pediatrician's office. Mom expected to get a firm diagnosis so they could get the problem fixed. Instead, she was told the situation demanded more testing. A referral was made and they were in the hearing clinic at the Oregon College of Education the next morning. Mom felt a gnawing fear in her stomach as they waited until the appointed time and were ushered into a soundproof booth specially designed to test people's hearing. Laura seemed happy, studying the toy monkey with his cymbals in one corner. There were additional displays of mechanical toys in other parts of the booth, which the audiologist could activate in the testing process. It took no time at all to discover that Laura had no awareness of sounds, but she delighted in the visual images she was seeing. A couple more tests and the specialist was ready to share her findings: Laura was profoundly deaf and it didn't seem like a problem that could be corrected surgically. She gave Mom the phone number for the parent/infant program at the school for the deaf. Then she was gone. Mom was stunned as she headed home, anxious to share the news with Dad so they could figure out how to handle this new problem.

Fortunately Tracy was at the house babysitting Phillip. Now she was waiting to take over with Laura. Mom handed the baby to her and collapsed on the sofa in tears. Tracy wasn't sure what to think so she took the kids to their bedrooms and engaged them in play while Mom gained enough composure to call Dad. "She's deaf, Bill. They say she's profoundly deaf and she'll need hearing aids to hear anything at all. What are we going to do?" she sobbed.

"Take it easy, Cheron. I'll ask around the hospital to see if anyone here has ideas. I just haven't had any experience with deaf children, or adults for that matter. I'll finish up my work and get home as soon as possible. Have Tracy help you with the kids."

Tracy did help with Phillip and Laura, a lot. Mom realized she was vulnerable because it was the anniversary of my death. Now this bad news about Laura sent her emotions out of control. She cried for most of two days and got very little sleep. Attempts to contact the program at the school for the deaf failed because everyone was on summer vacation.

When at last her tears were spent, a realization came to her that helped her get a grip: "She's deaf, not DEAD!" Gaining that perspective, she was able to separate the two kinds of grief she was experiencing. Her counselor training had taught her to sort out the factors causing stress so they could be managed more easily. "We may not know much about deafness now," she reasoned, "but we'll get ourselves educated so we can help Laura in whatever ways necessary. Heck, while DEAD doesn't give me much to work with, we can handle deafness." In the weeks that followed she borrowed books from the library. Dad had the hospital librarian run a search of the medical literature on childhood deafness. By September when the school year started and they were initiated into the parent/infant program, they had a basic understanding of the challenges ahead. They embarked on a new adventure in their lives.

37 Playground Dedication Day

The dedication of the Scotty Mayhall Memorial Playground was scheduled for August 27. All my family's major activity for the month was focused toward that end. It left little time to stew about Laura's deafness, though Mom and Dad were eager to read any helpful information they could get their hands on. Mom made fifty invitations for the dedication, enough to send to friends and family in the Northwest who could travel to Corvallis that day, and a few extras for people like my godparents and Texas grandparents who lived too far away to attend. The invitation was on blue parchment paper cut in the shape of the space capsule. The words on the cover indicated there would be a memorial and gave my full name and dates of my birth and death. Inside was a picture of me smiling, with the words:

> Please join us as we honor the memory of
> our beloved son
> at the dedication of the
> SCOTTY MAYHALL MEMORIAL PLAYGROUND,
> Little Beavers Preschool and Day Care,
> 4940 NW US Hwy. 99W, Corvallis, OR,
> Sunday, August 27, 1978, at 2 p.m.

Two weekends before the ceremony Dad located a flat-bed truck and four strong friends who helped hoist the capsule and spring wagon for the journey from our garage to the playground, thirty miles away. This crew met the owner, Al East, upon arrival, then the six of them used pulleys and wheels to position the equipment in place, one in front of the school and one in the back yard. The capsule was mounted on some bouncy box springs Mom found in a second-hand store. It bounced too much when several people got inside, so Dad crafted some feet to stabilize it on a bed of beauty bark. It was so cool, with an arched doorway and round windows. It sparkled silver in the summer sun.

Auntie Alice's family drove down from Seattle to be part of the work party two days before the Sunday ceremony. In addition to my cousins, David and Danny, who were big strong teenagers, Uncle Alex's oldest daughter, Angela, came to help. Angela was about the same age as the twins. She was born on Mom's birthday in October. Mom had a special place in her heart for this niece. It was also easy to remember Angela's birthday every year.

With all the family members and friends from Seattle and Salem, joining with Little Beavers supporters and friends from Corvallis, the work party was large so they got a lot done that Friday and Saturday, laboring until dark. My heavenly friends and I watched in wonder as the sections took shape. We were so happy for the fun and adventures Little Beavers students had in store. Besides the space capsule and climbing dome out front, they would play on the wagon and two-story fort out back, meeting for pow-wows in the teepee. The carpentry corral had some new tools. The bunnies had new cages. A rocking horse on springs had been added to the play yard near the slide and swing set.

The weather could not have been more perfect. Mom had made herself a new sundress. Laura wore a flowery dress of similar fabric, only Laura's had a white pinafore with eyelet ruffles for trim. Tied with ribbon beneath her chin was a frilly sun bonnet sent to her by Texas friends earlier in the spring. She looked like a baby doll. Phillip dressed in his new three-piece suit, blue and white pinstripes, but the day was very warm so he left the jacket on a hook inside Little Beavers. He still looked very snazzy in his long-sleeved white shirt, necktie and vest. Dad looked snazzy, too, dressed in a suit Mom made for him in a tailoring class she took the first year we lived in Oregon. A reporter from the newspaper was busy taking pictures and asking people to share memories of me and tell how they liked the new playground.

Mom had crafted a printed program for the occasion so people would know what to expect. This time the picture of my face was framed inside a heart that had a chunk missing near the point. Mom would explain about the chunk in her speech…how it symbolized that part of her heart was missing since I died.

Rev. McAmis served as pastor for the dedication, just as he had presided over my memorial service thirteen months earlier. He prayed at the beginning and end of the dedication, with speeches by Al East, Rhonda, Mom, Dad and Phillip sandwiched in between. The audience included about fifty children who were just itching to play on the equipment, even though many of them were dressed in Sunday school clothes. Their parents held their hands during the speeches so they would pay attention. Many of the adults were crying into their hankies so the kids knew it was a time to be still and listen, not to run around and yell.

When the serious part was over the kids cut loose to try out all the equipment, new and refurbished. Most of the adults talked with my parents while they enjoyed some refreshments being served under the awning of the carpentry corral. One of the Little Beavers moms had made an artistic plaque indicating that the playground was in memory of me. It was on a post near the entrance gate where everyone would see it. Alongside the words she had etched a pair of cowboy boots. People smiled as they remembered me in my boots. I smiled along with them.

Up in Heaven, Uncle Alex and GG talked with me and my friends about the importance of having created this memorial. It gave my family, as well as all their friends, a sense of completion to a year of sadness. We all felt the strength of the love link between

Heaven and Earth. The playground was a happy place which lifted people's spirits. It helped everyone to remember the way I laughed and loved and enjoyed life on Earth.

38 September Surprise

September arrived. The air seemed filled with the promise of new beginnings. Phillip could hardly wait to be back with his school friends and Mrs. Down in second grade.

The parent/infant program at the school for the deaf assigned a teacher to work with my whole family at our house. They were excited to start learning sign language and how to help Laura learn and grow. Mom found a brochure about the International Association of Parents of the Deaf. She joined and started receiving their helpful literature. The young teacher from the "PIP" program, Nancy, assured my folks that Laura would do just fine. Another teacher, Betty, was the first deaf adult my parents had ever met. She was amazingly competent and beautiful. Mom and Dad were encouraged that Baby Laura could grow up to be educated, independent, and happy like Betty. Nothing seemed to slow her down.

Mom had saved a secret to share with Dad on Labor Day. She told him with a twinkle in her eye, "Looks like that little operation you had last November is going to pay off. I've taken two home pregnancy tests and both came out positive. By my calculations, I will be experiencing 'labor day' sometime next spring!" They were both thrilled at the prospect of having another baby just a bit younger than Laura. They figured the two could grow up together, helping one another as they developed.

Steve and I were playing together in the heavenly treehouse when I felt a flash from my love link. "Wow!" I screamed with delight. "More baby news, Steve. My mom has a baby in her tummy too, just like yours. First Laura, then your new brother, then another baby coming to my family. God has really come through with the answers to our prayers. Babies, babies, everywhere. We gotta tell GG and the others. Now our families back on Earth are going to be getting bigger, and happier all the time."

Steve and I raced each other across the yard and into the kitchen. We got so excited telling our news that everyone in the house, upstairs and down, rushed to the kitchen to see about the commotion. When Uncle Alex heard the news he picked me up and tossed me in the air. "Hallelujah, praise the Lord! Earth and Heaven rejoice in unison."

Then he used the opportunity to invite everyone for a storytime he'd been planning. Each of us was invited to choose a favorite animal story. Unk would organize what he called an "animal storyfest." Depending on the number and length of the stories, it would last just one evening or continue for several. We'd sit comfortably around the big armchair in the far corner of our heavenly living room. Unk said he'd be happy to read some of the stories but encouraged us kids to take charge when we felt the urge. We could read stories or tell stories. Steve and I decided we'd like to act out a tale of Smokey the Bear that took place in the forest of New Mexico, since that was where I was born and lived as a baby.

Unk's idea was a great success. That first evening he read about "Jonah and the Whale" from the Bible. Gilberto also wanted to hear the Biblical story of "Daniel in the Lion's Den." Heather's favorite was a fairy tale by the Brothers Grimm called "The Wolf and Seven Goats." Steve, whose favorite story of all time was "Peter and the Wolf," was tickled to hear how this other bad wolf got fooled by a clever mother goat. There wasn't time for our Smokey show before treats and bedtime, but we were happy to save it for later. We'd practice. Maybe we'd make some costumes. GG and Lila had prepared frozen, chocolate-covered bananas on sticks. We all savored these treats at the end of a perfect family evening together, looking forward to an eternity of such happy moments.

Postscript

The playground dedication was an important turning point. It provided what modern-day therapists call "closure." Whereas acute grief work necessarily focuses on memories of the past and life with the lost beloved, the hardest task is to integrate those memories with the realities of the present as time marches on. The dedication signaled, initiated or allowed a realignment of priorities in which our bereaved family could move toward greater health and wholeness. Instead of feeling that life was prioritized past/present/future, the time had come to change the emphasis: to live fully in the present, to look with faith and anticipation toward the future, and to allow the unchangeable past to take third place in determining our thoughts and actions.

The memoir/novel is ended. What follows is a final tribute to Scotty – words spoken on the playground that day in August 1978. His short life left a lasting impression on the hearts of all who knew him.

Words of Remembrance, Playground Dedication Day

Mom "Searching for Sunlight Amidst Shadows of Sorrow"

To have suddenly lost a healthy, beautiful child – one as gifted and promising as was our Scotty – I am convinced that life can ask us to suffer no greater sorrow.

The death of a child violates the whole order of life – the logical, expected succession of the generations. No parent hopes to outlive his child. Scotty embodied many of our hopes and dreams for a lifetime, and his death has left us with loose ends.

For me, the sensation has been something more intense than a broken heart with painful cracks that will mend so that the heart will someday be whole again. It is more as if a chunk of my heart has completely fallen off. It is gone...irretrievably lost for a lifetime, leaving behind an anguish that will, in varying degrees, be felt forever.

For both Bill and me, our children are our most vulnerable point. We are strong, self-determined people, but to suffer over our children is the ultimate pain. I seriously doubt that time and circumstances will ever be such that we can honestly look back with satisfaction and understand the WHYS of Scotty's death. Nothing I can imagine will ever make it okay. Nothing will ever allow us to say, "Oh, that's the reason Scotty had to die" or "this or that person or experience was worth his life." A child is so precious!

I remember the words of Del McAmis at the memorial service last summer. He said, "Don't ask why…it can only lead to despair. There is no reasonable answer." And, when Rev. Henderlite visited in our home about a week after the funeral, I appreciated the fact that he didn't moralize or philosophize. I remember best his straightforward, caring statement, "You don't deserve this greatest of all sorrows. But, then, life isn't fair."

So we are left with the hard, cold truths: Scotty's death was neither reasonable nor fair. The reactions that come most overwhelmingly are despair, feelings of impotence and futility, and self-pity. None of them positive forces. Therefore, we have sought to put these behind us and to move in a more creative direction.

Our task has been, and continues to be, to transform the feelings of helplessness and hopelessness into faith, courage and zest for life. We hope we may glorify Scotty's sweet memory in the living of our lives.

There are so many wonderful things I could say about Scotty. He was a parent's and teacher's dream…a wonder and a joy to nurture. He was so loving and competent and creative. Most things came easy for him and we were constantly amazed at his keen abilities:

- He walked at 8 months
- By age 2 he was mastering puzzles
- He cut his own meat with precision at 3

- He wrote his whole name and tied his shoes with ease before turning 4
- He could whistle and he could wink

If something did prove difficult for him, he had such a strong will to succeed that he would work diligently until he had mastered the task.

Rhonda, his teacher, remarked to me that Scotty possessed a very mature moral sense. He seemed to have such a clear understanding of right and wrong. Disciplining him was made easy because he usually had a good idea of what was appropriate punishment, whether it be a period of quiet time away from others, or being assigned to a back room to tear the pages of an old telephone book in half in order to appease his desire to tear paper.

In his final year, his growth fostered by his excellent pre-school experience at Little Beavers, his genius was beginning to flower. If all this sounds idealistic, I do not apologize. To us, Scotty was an ideal child – much more wonderful than we had ever hoped for. Our mourning has been on three levels:

1) For Scotty himself, because he interacted so fully with his world and enjoyed life so very much.

2) For those closest who knew and loved him best – relatives, teachers, neighbors and a few special playmates. We are lonely for him.

3) For mankind and the world, because I believe with all my heart that Scotty would have contributed greatly and left his mark. Perhaps he <u>would</u> have been a spaceship commander —a pioneer on the frontier of his generation.

Because he was so wonderful to us, we want, in some way, to sustain the joy, happiness and creativity that <u>was</u> Scotty in life. So, we have searched these many months for some sunlight amidst the shadows of our sorrow. We have chosen to focus on our most joy-filled memories of Scotty, to recognize how much richer our lives are for having shared those few years with him.

The hopeful thing in my perception of this loss is illustrated inside your program: Though part of the heart is painfully missing, Scotty's spirit continues to permeate the part that remains. The strong love bond we share is eternal. His precious spirit will always shine through. Scotty inspires our search for sunlight. This playground memorial is a part of that search. In seeing his spirit perpetuated in the joy of other youngsters, we are comforted.

One ray of hopeful sunshine I'd especially like to mention: A dear friend said to me last weekend, "Out of your tragedy has grown my own increased awareness of how precious a gift our children are. I treasure every moment with them so much more."

Obviously this memorial could not have been possible without the help of scores of people. So many have contributed in terms of money, time and effort, and moral support. <u>We are so grateful.</u> I hesitate to name names on the chance of someone being offended if I omit his or her name. Yet, a few deserve special mention. Suffice it to say all of you who have been invited here today are recognized for your support. We appreciate you.

Special mention:
1) My mom, Bertha Messmer, who has suffered her own agony in losing her youngest grandchild, yet has sought to support us in every way she could.
2) My husband's folks, Temple and Mildred Mayhall, in Austin, Texas. They have known the frustration and loneliness of being so far away when we've all needed the mutual support families can give. Special thanks to Scotty's granddaddy for the love and talent he put into designing the space capsule.
3) Aunts, uncles and cousins – most especially Auntie Alice who loved Scotty as if he were her own son.
4) Jan and Al East who have allowed and encouraged this project. They have worked closely with us in all stages of planning and development.
5) The Little Beavers staff and their spouses. Also, the parents

who have helped, especially Cara Pence who has spent many hours working here and whose artistic handiwork can be seen on the space capsule and the commemorative plaque.
6) Our kind and supportive neighbors: Buhlers, Colgans, Easterlys, Payettes and Mulletts.
7) Wonderful friends we have known through our work in Salem and school at OSU: Boyds, Buzas, Chesters, Embicks, Devorss, Ellie Bohles, Pat Kinney, Langenbergs, Nelsons, Tripletts, Marilyn Johnston.
8) My precious friend, Satsuki Tomine, who came to be with us immediately upon hearing of Scotty's death. During that period, when we were trying to function in a state of shock, Satsuki helped us originate the idea for this memorial.
9) Our church friends, most especially the Wells, whose contributions in terms of money, work and moral support have been most generous. And to Sylvia Kline who had the courage to reach out to me on two occasions when I needed to talk or weep about my loss.
10) Many others, too numerous to name – we are grateful to all who have made this day possible.

If Scotty were here to see this playground and to spend this afternoon with all of you, he would be brimming over with happiness. Let us think of him that way, and let us dedicate this memorial with remembrances of the joy that was our Scotty. Let his spirit shine through our hearts as sunlight to dispel the dark shadows.

Teacher, Rhonda "Remembering Scotty"

As Scotty's teacher, certain memories of him are most vivid. I see him with his cowboy boots, two or three belts and ropes – which he so ingeniously used in all types of imaginative play. He of course shared his treasured accessories with his "best friends" as he called them. I recall Scotty drawing a rocketship for his placemat which he so precisely sketched and colored, along with verbally naming each part. I was amazed and hurriedly showed the other teachers and his mother when she picked him up.

Dinosaurs were a big hit with Scotty and he made it spectacular for the whole group with his "show-n-tell" items from home. He taught us <u>all</u> about dinosaurs. When Dr. Mayhall came to visit, our housekeeping area was quickly converted to a hospital with lots of patients and the "new" Dr. Mayhall assisting.

I have recently reread the book, <u>The Little Prince</u>, by Saint-Exupery. So many parts of it remind me of Scotty. For those of you who have read the book and know Scotty, I'm sure you know what I mean. To me he truly was, and still is, a "free spirit" so uniquely imaginative and creative. I am happy that some of Scotty's ideas and goals, from cowboys to astronauts, can now be shared in structural form with many little friends, stimulating growth and imagination.

Father and Brother (Leading the audience in unison)

"Words of Dedication"

We, here assembled, now dedicate this playground to the memory of Scotty Mayhall. May his spirited laughter and creative energy be reflected in the happy, carefree play of other small children for many years to come.

Bibliography

Agee, James *A Death in the Family*. Vintage Books (a division of Random House), New York, 1957.

Gunther, John *Death Be Not Proud – A Memoir*. Harper & Row, Perennial Library, New York, 1949.

Kubler-Ross, Elisabeth *On Death and Dying*. MacMillan, New York, 1969.

Kubler-Ross, Elisabeth *Questions and Answers on Death and Dying*. MacMillan, New York, 1974.

Mayhall, Cheron J. *The Development of a Methodology to Study the Grief and Adjustment Processes of Parents Following the Death of a Young Child*. Doctoral dissertation, Oregon State University, Corvallis, 1982.

Miller, Arthur *All My Sons - A Drama in Three Acts*. Penguin Twentieth Century Classics, New York, 1947.

Moustakas, Clark *Loneliness and Love*. Simon & Schuster, New York, 1972.

Saint-Exupery, Antoine de *The Little Prince*. Harcourt, Inc., New York, 1943.

Sarnoff-Schiff, Harriet *The Bereaved Parent*. Crown Publishers, Inc., New York, 1977.

Stephens, Simon *Death Comes Home*. Morehouse-Barlow Co., New York, 1973.

Tazewell, Charles *The Littlest Angel*. Childrens Press, Inc., Chicago, 1946.

White, William Allen *The Autobiography of William Allen White*, MacMillan, New York, 1946.

Wilder, Thornton *The Bridge of San Luis Rey*, Washington Square Press/Simon & Schuster, New York, 1927. (Copyright, 1927, by Albert & Charles Boni, Inc. Copyright renewed, 1955, by Thornton Wilder. Current publishing rights controlled by HarperCollins.)

A Path through Grief Work to Healing

- Accept the reality of the loss. Until you begin to make peace with it, you cannot move ahead to other stages of recovery.

- The pain can be diminished by talking about your feelings and experiences. Find a relative, a friend or another confidant who is a good listener.

- There will be waves of emotion beyond your control that may arise when you least expect them. Go with the ebb and flow. Tears are cleansing. Expressions of anger can help diffuse pent-up pain.

- Re-engage in social life, but realize that your role has changed, e.g. bereaved parent, widow or widower. You need other people who can help fill the void left by the lost loved one.

- As soon as possible, return to your involvement in the community, church, synagogue, etc. You may need to force yourself, but it's necessary to healing and health.

- Search for meaning in the loss. You will be profoundly changed through the experience. Most people find strength they didn't know they had. They learn how to handle pain and aloneness. They discover their own path to healing. These new capacities carry over into other areas of your life.

Quick Order Form

Fax orders: 250 383 6804
           Send this form.

Phone orders: Call 250 383 6864 (toll free 1 888 232 4444)
           Have credit card ready.

Email orders: orders@trafford.com

Postal orders: Trafford Publishing, 6E – 2333 Government St
                       Victoria, BC   V8T 4P4

Please send book(s): _____ *@ $21.24/each*

Name:_____

Address:_____

City:_____ State/Province:_____

Zip/Postal Code:_____

Telephone:_____

Email address: _____

*Cost for book, plus shipping and handling:*_____

Payment: ❏ Check   ❏ Credit Card

                ❏ VISA   ❏ Master Card

Card number:_____
Name on Card:_____
Exp. Date:_____

Signature of Cardholder:_____

About the Author

Photo by Dusty Westall

After the sudden death of her young son, Dr. Mayhall made the long journey through grief to joy. Since 1977, both her personal and professional life have been influenced by the need and desire to survive and thrive beyond intense sorrow. In the process, she has successfully helped others do the same.

Following her 1960's Peace Corps experience, working with toddlers and their impoverished families in Honduras, Cheron became a counselor and medical social worker in Texas and New Mexico. At the time of her child's death she was studying for her Ph.D. in Counseling and Adult Education at Oregon State University. Her doctoral research and dissertation explores the characteristics that contribute to parental healing after the death of a child.

She was founder and President of the Salem, Oregon chapter of The Compassionate Friends, an international organization supporting bereaved parents and families. In 1983-84 she founded the Coalition in Oregon for Parent Education (COPE) where she served for thirteen years as Executive Director. This statewide organization provides education to support families raising children with disabilities. These families grieve and despair; it was COPE's mission to give them hope with the skills to survive.

Cheron served on the Board of the National Parent Network on Disability. She was President of the American Society for Deaf Children (ASDC) from 1999 to 2002. In 2005 she received ASDC's most prestigious honor, the Lee Katz Award.

Cheron lives with her husband and pets in Port Townsend,